A Classroom Teacher's Guide to Struggling Readers

Curt Dudley-Marling
and
Patricia C. Paugh

Heinemann
Portsmouth, NH

Heinemann
A division of Reed Elsevier Inc.
361 Hanover Street
Portsmouth, NH 03801–3912
www.heinemann.com

Offices and agents throughout the world

The authors and publisher wish to thank those who have generously given permission to reprint borrowed material:

Chapter 8: The transcript of the short story discussion between Mr. Jones and his fourth graders was taken from a video made by the Institute for Learning (IFL) at the University of Pittsburgh in collaboration with the Great Books Foundation. The video footage will be used on the IFL's *Developing Norms* CD-ROM as part of the *Accountable Talk: Classroom Conversation That Works* suite of tools. We are indebted to Sarah Michaels, from Clark University, for making this transcript available for our use.

Library of Congress Cataloging-in-Publication Data
Dudley-Marling, Curt.
    A classroom teacher's guide to struggling readers / Curt Dudley-Marling and Patricia C. Paugh.
        p. cm.
    Includes bibliographical references and index.
    ISBN 0-325-00541-9 (alk. paper)
    1. Reading (Elementary). 2. Reading—Remedial teaching. I. Paugh, Patricia C., 1956–. II. Title.
LB1573.D74 2004
372.43—dc22   2004010518

Editor: Lois Bridges
Production: Elizabeth Valway
Cover design: Joni Doherty
Cover art of miscue is from Miscue Analysis Made Easy *by Sandra Wilde*
Composition: Tom Allen/Pear Graphic Design
Manufacturing: Steve Bernier

Printed in the United States of America on acid-free paper
08 07 06 05 04   RRD   1 2 3 4 5

Contents

Acknowledgments

We wish to acknowledge Maura Lunney, from the Holyoke Massachusetts Public Schools, and Andrea Florence, Shelley Russell, Valerie King-Jackson, Marlene Peppin, Jo-Anne Wilson-Keenan, and Jessica Auriello, of the Springfield Massachusetts Public Schools, for letting us include some of their work in this book. We also wish to acknowledge Mary Kim Fries, of the University of New Hampshire, the coauthor of the *Wild Things* lesson. We wish to thank Lois Bridges, our editor at Heinemann, for her encouragement, support, feedback, and most of all kindness. Finally, we want to thank our families, Jim and Jimmy Paugh and Chris, Anne, and Ian Dudley-Marling, for their patience and support.

Asking and Answering the Tough Questions

This book is about teaching struggling readers—students for whom reading and learning to read are especially difficult. Some of these students have acquired learning disability labels and receive special instruction in resource rooms. Other struggling readers receive remedial assistance through programs like Title I or Reading Recovery. Many struggling readers, however, receive no special assistance and depend on the instruction their classroom teachers are able to provide.

What struggling readers have in common is the need for "frequent, intensive, explicit, and individualized support and direction" (Rhodes and Dudley-Marling 1996) informed by careful, ongoing assessment. The challenge for teachers is to create structures that enable them to provide the individualized support and direction struggling readers require. These same structures allow teachers to routinely collect the assessment data needed to provide reading instruction that responds to the specific instructional needs of *all* their students—struggling readers *and* the most able.

In this book, we show classroom teachers how they can support struggling readers via the organization of time and space inherent in a reading workshop. We present a wide range of effective instructional strategies. We also consider how commercial reading programs can be adapted to better meet the needs of struggling readers. But, however organized, instruction must be linked to appropriate, ongoing assessment; therefore, throughout this book we detail assessment strategies that produce the rich data needed to plan appropriate instruction for struggling readers.

Let's begin with some questions and answers about the "big ideas" of working with struggling readers.

Why can't Jeremy read?

We want to be clear—we explicitly reject deficit models that pathologize struggling readers by situating learning problems *in the heads of individual learners*. There's little point or value in attributing reading difficulties to learning disabilities, attention deficits, or dyslexia, for example—these labels do not lead directly or automatically to any particular instructional strategies. Nor is there any evidence that remedial or special education students—or any other struggling readers—have *unique* instructional needs demanding reading instruction that is qualitatively different from instruction provided to their more academically successful peers (Rhodes and Dudley-Marling 1996). Struggling readers are, however, more likely than their peers to require reading instruction that is *intensive*, *explicit*, and *individualized*.

The question for us is not, *what's wrong with Jeremy?* but rather, what does Jeremy need to learn in order to continue his development as a reader and what can we do to support his reading development? The key to this support is careful, routine assessment that seeks to identify what struggling readers already know about language and literacy as the foundation on which reading instruction will build.

What are the primary goals for teaching struggling readers?

The primary goal for teachers of reading must be to push *all* their students as far as they can go as readers. Struggling readers progress by learning the skills and strategies more proficient readers use as they work to make sense of different kinds of texts. Struggling readers learn, for example, how to use sound-symbol relationships, predictable grammatical structures, and their knowledge of the world to make sense of texts. They learn comprehension strategies like predicting, skimming, visualizing, and rereading. They also learn to relate what they are reading to their personal experience, background knowledge, and other texts. Struggling readers do not, however, learn to read "once and for all" (Gee 1991), since different purposes and genres demand different skills and strategies. Therefore, effective teachers of struggling readers offer the support and direction students need to read *as wide a range of genres* (realistic fiction, historical fiction, fantasy, nonfiction, biography) for *as wide a range of purposes* (reading for pleasure, for literary experiences, for information, to perform a task) as possible.

Goals set for individual struggling readers must reflect state and local language arts frameworks; state- and district-mandated reading tests; the recommended standards of professional associations like the International Reading Association (IRA) and the National Council of Teachers of English (NCTE); and, most important, careful, ongoing assessment. The *Massachusetts English Language Arts Curriculum Framework* (Massachusetts Department of Education 2001), for example, states that in first and second grades students should learn to "make predictions about the content of a text using prior knowledge and text features . . . and explain whether they were confirmed or disconfirmed and why." This is a reasonable expectation for all readers, but classroom teachers need to determine the appropriateness of this goal for individual first and second graders through their ongoing assessment of the students' reading development. Still, even a struggling reader who cannot read text independently may be able to "make and evaluate" predictions of texts that are read to him.

Which approaches to reading instruction work best for struggling readers?

Arguably, a book for teachers about struggling readers ought to focus on instructional strategies that have been *proven* to work with students for whom learning to read is a struggle, especially given the emphasis on "scientifically based" instruction in the No Child Left Behind Act.

But *which approaches to reading instruction work best for struggling readers?* is the wrong question. First, as we have already argued, it is doubtful that the instructional needs of struggling readers are unique. Further, *what works?* needs to be qualified by *at what? for whom?* and *compared to what?* A strategy deemed to "work" because it helps children sound out nonsense words, for example, may have little effect on reading comprehension.

Similarly, it is generally unhelpful to know that a strategy "works" for a generic group of students, as determined by "scientific research." Ordinarily, a reading strategy or method is declared *effective* or *research-based* on the strength of statistical comparisons of average performances of two or more groups, one of which has been instructed using the method being touted. However, such comparisons reference *average* performance only, and teachers work with individual children, not statistically constructed average children. Further, claims of effectiveness, because they are based on comparisons between relatively small numbers of programs or strategies, are always limited. No matter how well students taught using program A perform compared to students taught with program B or program C, no claims can be made about program A relative to programs D, E, or F if these programs were not part of the original comparison.

In any case, no reading method, no matter how many studies are cited to assert its effectiveness, has ever been found to "work" with all students, in all settings, all the time (e.g., Allington and Johnston 2001; Dykstra 1968; Pearson 1997). As Duffy and Hoffman (1999) put it, "no single method or approach has ever been proven to be a cure-all" (11). Certainly, research offers general guidance for teachers as they design appropriate instruction for children in their classrooms, but individual teachers must determine what works by carefully monitoring their instruction of individual children. Therefore, routine assessment of children's reading development must include ongoing appraisal of how children respond to various instructional strategies. In the end, teachers are accountable for their performance and the performance of their students; specifically, they must provide concrete evidence to parents and supervisors that they made appropriate instructional decisions—based on careful, ongoing assessment—that pushed each child in their classroom as far as he or she could go as a reader. It would be ludicrous for teachers to claim they are providing appropriate instruction merely by pointing to research evidence supporting the instructional strategies they have selected without demonstrating how these strategies worked with individual children in their classroom.

How do I find the time to provide "individualized support and direction" for struggling readers?

Time is crucial for already overburdened teachers, who are well within their rights to resist taking on "one more thing." The only way to address the needs of struggling readers successfully is by creating classroom structures that enable teachers to do ongoing assessment and provide students with frequent, intensive, explicit, and individualized support and direction as needed without adding to the already overwhelming demands of teaching. Our preferred approach to creating organizational space congenial to the diverse needs of struggling readers is a reading workshop. In a reading workshop teachers can address the individual needs of all their students without expending unreasonable amounts of time. Since many teachers are required to follow basal reading programs, we also suggest ways to adapt them to be more considerate of the needs of struggling readers.

Do struggling readers need more structure?

All learners, including struggling readers, require predictable, well-ordered learning environments. All students also benefit from some degree of explicit and individualized support and direction. The International Reading Association (IRA) has declared that every student has a "right" to appropriate reading instruction based on his or her "individual needs" (IRA 2000). Effective teachers carefully structure time and learning spaces in their classrooms in order to meet the various learning needs of their students. To the degree that struggling readers are more likely to require "frequent, intense, explicit, and individualized support and direction," structure is especially important.

It all depends, however, on the meaning of *structure*. Teachers need to structure time and space in their classrooms to support struggling readers. Too often, however, structure equates with fragmented, decontextualized skill instruction. This kind of structure benefits no student, especially a struggling reader, who requires instruction in a context that routinely demonstrates that reading is always meaningful and active (Smith 1998).

What does "frequent, intensive, explicit, and individualized support and direction" mean?

All students require some individual support and direction, and we expect struggling readers to need more of it than their classmates. Similarly, all students benefit from some form of *explicit* instruction, and, again, struggling readers will be more likely to require this direct instruction.

Most children come to school having learned a great deal about what readers do when they read. They generally know how to orient books. They have learned that the pages of a book must be turned from front to back. They have made the discovery that print represents meaning. Most also have developed at least a rudimentary sense that letters represent sound. A relatively smaller number of children come to school as fluent readers.

In most cases, the knowledge children acquire about reading before they come to school comes from being read to by their parents and from their own experience with books and other sources of print (signs, labels, etc.). In contrast, school-based literacy instruction often focuses on explicit skills, separate from the reading of books. Although struggling readers do require some explicit instruction in the skills and strategies used by mature readers, such instruction should generally be embedded in a rich program of reading a wide variety of texts (Allington 2000). An overemphasis on decontextualized skill instruction is tedious and denies emerging readers vital information about how reading skills and strategies are used in the context of reading texts. (Examples of how teachers provide explicit instruction within the context of meaningful reading are provided throughout this book.)

Will a reading workshop lead to chaos and confusion in my classroom?

For many parents, administrators, and teachers, center- or workshop-based classrooms conjure up images of children wandering from place to place, perhaps reading, perhaps chatting with friends or daydreaming, perhaps participating in required activities, perhaps just fooling around, perhaps talking about the books they're reading, perhaps gossiping or talking about their favorite TV programs. In short, we worry that if we allow too much freedom of movement in the classroom, we will lose control of both our students' learning and our sanity.

There are, certainly, reading workshops in which the children are "out of control" or at least have not been given sufficient direction. But more often, reading workshops—whether in well-funded or poorly funded schools—are planned, well-organized sessions in which students are actively engaged in a range of profitable reading experiences. Successful reading workshops are run by teachers who carefully organize time and space in their classroom: the physical space is thoughtfully laid out, and reading activities are both meaningful and consistent with children's developmental needs. But most important, successful reading workshops are set up by teachers who take the time to teach their students the routines. Attention to routines is vital.

Should I teach phonics or not?

Teachers—and the general public—have been led to believe that there is a *war* going on (i.e., the "reading wars") for the hearts and minds of teachers between educators who favor the teaching of phonics and those who do not. This is a false and grossly misleading dichotomy. All reputable reading educators and researchers acknowledge an important role for phonics in the reading process and in early reading instruction. No one imagines that children or adults read with their eyes closed, as if the print on the page doesn't matter. Children and adult readers all attend to the print on the page; therefore, decoding is a crucial aspect of reading. There are, however, differences among reading educators over *how*, *when*, and *why* students are taught phonics.

It is generally agreed that explicit teaching of phonics skills is necessarily a part of early reading instruction, but, again, there are strong differences of opinion about the nature of this instruction. Most reading educators take the position, supported by research, that teaching children how English orthography works—sometimes explicitly—*must* be part of early reading instruction. However, an exclusive emphasis on the orthographic aspects of reading denies struggling readers access to other linguistic cues that are always part of the process. Even the two federally sponsored reports that are most often cited in support of explicit phonics instruction—*Preventing Reading Difficulties in Young Children* (Snow, Burns, and Griffin 1998) and *Teaching Children to Read* (National Reading Panel 2000)—are clear that such instruction *must be embedded in a rich and varied program of reading* (Garan 2002; Pearson 2001).

Should I group students for instruction?

Although whole-class activities are often useful, a heavy emphasis on whole-class instruction is rarely congenial to the needs of diverse learners. Meeting the varied needs of individual learners requires both individual and small-group activities. Grouping by ability, however, frequently has a significant negative effect on the learning of students placed in lower reading groups (Opitz 1999). Children in the lower groups rarely experience the same range of reading opportunities as do students in the higher groups, which may explain why students often don't progress from lower to higher reading groups (Hiebert 1983). Therefore, we strongly recommend flexible, short-term, heterogeneous groupings that bring students together to learn particular skills, read common texts, or work cooperatively on projects (Caldwell and Ford 2002; Opitz 1999).

Asking and Answering the Tough Questions

Reading Workshop

A Structure That Supports All Students

T here's nothing like a real-life example. Mr. Garcia's third-grade reading workshop proceeds like this: he begins by *reading aloud* to his students, after which he presents a *whole-class minilesson* on some aspect of reading. Students then have a significant block of time for *independent reading* and *small-group activities,* followed by *self-assessment.* Let's step into his classroom and watch.

Reading Aloud

Mr. Garcia signals the beginning of reading workshop by reading *Baseball Saved Us,* by Ken Mochizuki (1995), a powerful fictionalized account of a Japanese American family and their internment during World War II. The students are moved by this story, and after he finishes many of them share their feelings about the injustice of the internment camps. Mr. Garcia steers the discussion to racism generally.

Minilesson

During earlier reading conferences Mr. Garcia has observed that many of his third graders, especially his struggling readers, fail to draw on their background knowledge and personal experience to help them make sense of what they read. He wants to explicitly teach his students strategies for making connections between texts they are reading and their background knowledge and experience—how to make text-to-self (relating texts to your own experiences), text-to-world (relating texts to knowledge you have about the larger world), and text-to-text (relating texts to other texts you've read) connections (Keene and Zimmerman 1997).

He introduces the notion of making text connections by using the story he has just read aloud. He tells the class, "While reading this story I started thinking about when I was a boy and some of the discrimination I faced. When I was in high school, whenever my friends and I went shopping in the drugstore downtown, the manager would follow us around, making sure we didn't steal anything. I think he didn't trust us because we were teenagers, and I thought that was unfair. I'm going to read the story again. As you listen, think about how the story connects to your own experiences."

Early in the story Mr. Garcia pauses and shares what he's thinking about what he's just read. He labels this a "text-to-self" connection and briefly explains the concept. At several other predetermined places in the text, he again stops and shares what he is thinking. When he finishes, he invites his students to share what they have been thinking about as he read to them. He records their responses on a flipchart, using what they offer to further explain the notion of text-to-self connections.

(Over the next several weeks, Mr. Garcia presents additional mini-lessons on making text-to-self, text-to-text, and text-to-world connections when reading narrative texts. He routinely follows up these whole-class minilessons with more extended individual and small-group instruction for students most in need of these strategies. Later in the year he helps his students make similar connections to expository texts.)

Independent Reading/Small-Group Activities

The furniture in Mr. Garcia's classroom is flexibly arranged (see Figure 1.1), and there is print everywhere. His students move around freely.

Today, several students read favorite books while leaning against pillows in the reading center, a carpeted corner of the room bound by bookcases filled with books and magazines. Two other students are listening to a recorded story while following along in copies of the book. Two boys sit on the floor while a girl named Crystal reads Shel Silverstein poems to them. Five children sit on the carpet discussing and sharing scary stories they've been reading, children's versions of *Dracula*, *Frankenstein*, *Dr. Jeckyl and Mr. Hyde,* and various titles from R. L. Stine's Goosebumps series. Two students seated at a table near the science center talk quietly as they page through magazines they've brought from home. A boy named Mark reads and writes notes at the message center next to Mr. Garcia's desk. Five or six students read quietly at desks and tables around the classroom, and a girl named Sophie has found a quiet spot to read by herself just outside the classroom door. Two

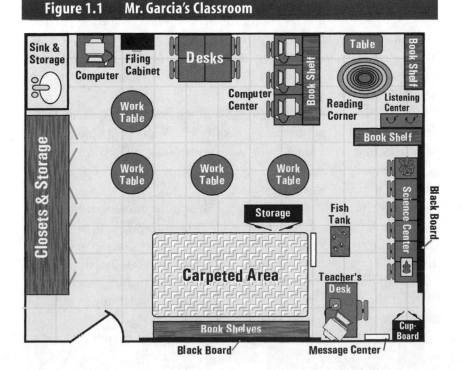

Figure 1.1   Mr. Garcia's Classroom

other girls stand at the blackboard reading out loud poems and song lyrics displayed on posted charts.

As his students get down to work, Mr. Garcia helps Charles, who often has trouble locating books appropriate to his reading ability and interests, find a book to read. Then he conducts a guided reading lesson with four struggling readers—Charles, Tasha, Emmet, and Ali. The goal of guided reading is to help children use independent reading strategies successfully. Typically, teachers work with a small group of students around a common text

> that offers children a minimum of new things to learn. . . . The focus is primarily on constructing meaning while using problem-solving strategies to figure out words they don't know, deal with tricky sentence structure, and understand concepts or ideas they have not previously met in print. The idea is for children to take on novel texts, read them at once with a minimum of support, and read many of them again and again for independence and fluency. (Fountas and Pinnell 1996, 2)

Today Mr. Garcia's guided reading lesson focuses on the text-to-self connections introduced during the minilesson. He reads the first several pages of *The Stories Julian Tells* (Cameron 1989), occasionally pausing to ask, "What were you thinking as I was reading to you?" When these initial efforts to stimulate discussion meet with silence, Mr. Garcia asks, "Can anyone tell me about fibs they've told? Or maybe you can think of a time you told a story that exaggerated something that really happened?" This question gets the discussion going, and Mr. Garcia talks again about how text-to-self connections help readers understand what they are reading.

After he finishes with the guided reading group, Mr. Garcia joins a literature-sharing group made up of five of his most capable readers, who have been reading *Frindle* (Clements 1998). Literature-sharing groups provide a social context for reading as a means of deepening students' comprehension.

Next Mr. Garcia conducts a series of reading conferences with individual students. As he talks with each one about what he or she has been reading, he takes notes: the story Tony has chosen to read is too difficult for him; Natalie, perhaps for the first time, has drawn an inference from the story she is reading. He also takes *running records* (see Chapter 4) as he listens to three of his students read orally in order to assess the text-processing strategies they use.

Mr. Garcia also works individually with several struggling readers.

Because Melissa's oral reading is slow and halting, he reads a text out loud with her (assisted reading). He reads smoothly and evenly, providing a fluent model. He lowers his voice slightly when Melissa controls the text and raises it again when she falters. Mr. Garcia then asks Melissa to read the same text over and over (repeated reading) until she can read the text independently. (Combined assisted and repeated reading is a particularly powerful strategy for increasing students' reading fluency [Rhodes and Dudley-Marling 1996].) Next, Mr. Garcia spends several minutes helping Kevin make better use of contextual cues when reading. Whenever Kevin miscues Mr. Garcia asks, "Does this make sense?" Finally, Mr. Garcia helps Kimberly recognize orthographic cues that signal whether a vowel is long (*māte*) or short (*măt* or *mătter*).

He spends the few remaining minutes conducting quick conferences with George, Jennifer, and Crystal, discussing what each is reading and what, if any, problems he or she is having.

In the meantime, several students have rotated in and out of the reading corner. The students in the guided reading group are now doing a word sort Mr. Garcia had prepared for them. (He often uses word sorts to help his students "develop the habit of analyzing words to look for patterns" [Cunningham 2000, 111]. Usually, he asks students to look at a group of words—written on cards—and sort them into categories based on spelling patterns, sound, or meaning.) The word sort Mr. Garcia has prepared today includes words like *rain, cat, name,* and *saw;* he hopes they will draw his students' attention to orthographic features that signal a long or short vowel.

The two girls who were reading poems and song lyrics are now reading independently, while the four children who had been reading quietly by themselves have (at Mr. Garcia's signal) resumed a discussion of a book they had been reading together. Joel, Sophie, Natalie, Crystal, and Graham, the students who had been discussing *Frindle,* move to the computer center to continue their Internet research on the author, Andrew Clements.

There have been, to be sure, several disruptions during this portion of the reading workshop, and considerable persuasion has been required to get Charles to do any reading at all. But, on balance, these third graders, many of whom are struggling readers, have been actively reading. Mr. Garcia does not, however, take student engagement for granted. His daily lesson plans structure his time as well as that of his students (see Figure 1.2). An organizational chart indicates weekly

Figure 1.2   Sample Lesson Plan

LESSON PLAN: Monday, November 18

8:45   Read-aloud: *Baseball Saved Us*

9:00   Minilesson (GOAL: Reading comprehension: making text-to-self connections)

- Say what I was thinking about while I was reading aloud. Tell students that I'm going to reread *Baseball Saved Us*.
- Reread *Baseball Saved Us*.
- Stop at a place early in the text and share what I was thinking about as I was reading. Tell students this is a text-to-self connection and explain what that means.
- Tell students that when I finish reading I will ask them to make their own text-to-self connections.
- Finish story. Ask students for text-to-self connections. Model further from my own experience if necessary. Record student responses on a flipchart.
- Discuss the text-to-self connections on the chart with the class.

9:10   Independent reading/small-group activities

<u>What I'll be doing</u>

- Help Charles find a book; make sure everyone is settled.
- Guided reading (Charles, Tasha, Emmet, Ali): Extend minilesson on text-to-self connections using *The Stories Julian Tells*. Read first few pages myself, stopping occasionally and asking, "What were you thinking as I was reading?" Maybe begin by asking group to talk about fibs they've told or stories where they've exaggerated.
- Literature-sharing group (Joel, Sophie, Natalie, Crystal, Graham): Continue discussion of *Frindle*. Extend today's minilesson by emphasizing text-to-self connections, then introduce text-to-text connections by asking students if *Frindle* reminds them of other books they've read. Label these text-to-text connections. Use chart to keep track of examples and, eventually, label the chart.
- Observe closely: Do running records with Andrea, Sarah, Michael (using whatever they're reading).
- Reading conferences/individual lessons: Melissa (assisted/repeated reading); Tamim (assisted/repeated reading); Robert (using contextual cues: "Does this make sense?"); Kimberly (recognizing orthographic cues: long and short vowels).
- Quick reading conferences today: Tony, Kevin, George.

Figure 1.2   Sample Lesson Plan continued

<u>Student Schedule</u>

This week's groupings:

> <u>Green</u>: Andrea, Sarah, Michael, Kevin, Tony, George
> <u>Blue</u>: Joel, Sophie, Natalie, Crystal, Graham
> <u>Yellow</u>: Charles, Tasha, Emmet, Ali
> <u>Orange</u>: Melissa, Robert, Kimberly, Tamim
> <u>Red</u>: Peter, Mark, Jennifer, Kristen, Linda

Today:

> <u>Green</u>: Reading conferences with me; independent reading; author study; reading evaluation
> <u>Blue</u>: Literature-sharing group; continue with author study; independent reading; reading evaluation
> <u>Yellow</u>: Guided reading; word sort; follow-up activity to shared reading: scanning a picture book chosen from the classroom library and using sticky notes to identify text-to-self connections; independent reading; reading evaluation
> <u>Orange</u>: Cloze task; author study; reading conferences with me; independent reading; reading evaluation
> <u>Red</u>: Independent reading; reading evaluation

10:00   Self-evaluation. Ask each group to reflect on what they have learned from their activities, check to see if the literature-sharing group and the guided reading students have completed student assessment forms

10:05   Whole-group debriefing. Be sure to ask if anyone had problems with their reading today.

groupings and daily expectations for students. Groupings are flexible, based on students' needs and interests, and therefore tend to be heterogeneous and to change frequently. One of the reasons Mr. Garcia and his students are so productive during independent reading is that Mr. Garcia taught these classroom routines during the first month of school. On this day in November, students are able to manage their time responsibly.

Immersing Students in Print

Mr. Garcia's students' active engagement with print is sustained by an inviting array of books, magazines, and other print resources. The classroom bookshelves are filled with literally hundreds of books—fiction, nonfiction, picture books, "chapter" books, music books, joke books, collections of children's poetry—organized by genre. Many are displayed, covers visible, along the blackboard chalk trays, on the tops of bookshelves and cabinets, and inside the bookcases at the front of the room. There is also a shelf of "easy to read" books. Books the students have created are displayed along the chalk tray in the back of the classroom. Since the class is in the middle of a month long study of folktales, numerous books of folktales, many gathered from the school and public libraries, are displayed atop the bookshelves in the front of the room. The reading center contains books, audiotapes (most read by students and parent volunteers), magazines (*Ranger Rick*, *National Geographic*, *Sports Illustrated for Kids*, *Time for Kids*), old encyclopedias, and catalogues. Additional books are stored on the shelves above the coat closets. Mr. Garcia regularly rotates his stock, so that the books on display are fresh and inviting.

The walls and blackboards of Mr. Garcia's classroom are covered with "environmental print," which he hopes will engage his students. Because he plays the guitar and frequently sings songs with his class, he has copied song lyrics onto chart paper and taped them on the blackboard. Mr. Garcia often shares poetry with his students, and many favorites are displayed on the doors of the coat closets. Recent examples of student writing are displayed in locations throughout the room. Jokes and comics students have brought from home are taped to the classroom door. A piece Mr. Garcia has written during a minilesson to illustrate how writers insert text in their writing is exhibited on the easel next to his desk. Charts that remind students of reading strategies discussed during minilessons—suggestions for choosing appropriate books, advice on what to do when encountering an unknown word—are also prominently displayed.

Returning to Mr. Garcia's classroom a few weeks later, we would find different poems, songs, jokes, rhymes, and student work on the classroom walls. Mr. Garcia routinely refreshes the environmental print in his classroom to make sure his students continue to find it inviting. He also regularly assesses whether his students are reading the print on the classroom walls. For example, when a series of articles about a local basketball tournament didn't generate much interest, he replaced them with something else.

Self-Assessment

The independent reading portion of Mr. Garcia's reading workshop always culminates in a written self-assessment that helps him and his students remain aware of how they are using their time in relation to the goals of each language arts activity. Mr. Garcia has his students complete a form that asks the following questions:

- What did I read today?
- What else did I do?
- Did I encounter any problems?
- What do I need to do to become a better reader?

He also routinely conducts a whole-class review of independent reading. Today the students in the literature-sharing group present some highlights of their discussion, and the students who took part in the guided reading lesson review the strategies they used to make meaning from the text. Other students share what they've been reading, pointing out particularly interesting language. Linda, Graham, and Sarah give the titles and authors of new books they've started. Kimberly and Peter are further along in the books they began the previous week.

Tamim recounts an amusing incident from *Skinnybones* (Park 1982). When Mr. Garcia asks if anyone had any problems with their reading, Kevin raises his hand: "I was reading a section of *Dr. Jekyl and Mr. Hyde* to the students at my table. When I read, 'Mr. Hyde walked on the man,' Tony repeated it and said it didn't sound right. So I reread the sentence and found my mistake. There was a period between 'walked on' and 'the man.' I should have read, 'Mr. Hyde walked on. The man. . . .'"

Mr. Garcia's efforts to create a literacy learning environment in which his students have extended interactions with print and to carefully support and direct his students' continuing literacy development are not left to chance. Based on his ongoing assessment of his students, Mr. Garcia develops detailed lesson plans that indicate both what he will do during independent reading and the nature of the independent work he expects his students to complete. Overall, Mr. Garcia's organized approach to time and space in his classroom enables him to immerse his students in print while providing "frequent, intensive, explicit, and individualized support and direction" as determined by routine assessment of his students' literacy development.

Creating Print-Rich Classrooms

Classrooms that support struggling readers immerse students in print that both invites students to read for extended periods and reflects a range of genres: fiction, nonfiction, song books, picture books, magazines, newspapers, comics, dictionaries, encyclopedias, signs, labels, computer software, letters, and notes.

Environmental Print

The strategic use of environmental print gives students more things to read and demonstrates the high value teachers place on literacy. Environmental print may be particularly attractive to struggling readers, whose experiences with books have not always been positive. Examples of environmental print include:

- Charts of poems, songs, and minilessons.
- Lists, signs, graphs, lunch menus, attendance sheets, job lists, and labels.
- Wish lists of books students would like in their classroom library or topics students are interested in reading about.
- Student biographies, birthdays.

- Charts listing strategies for choosing books, coping with unknown words, organizing writing (e.g., semantic webs), etc.
- Directions for various activities/materials.
- Classroom rules (e.g., rules for appropriate behavior during reading workshop).
- Samples of student work.
- Stories, articles, jokes, and comics.
- A word wall of frequently used words (see Cunningham 2000).
- Message boards.
- Web pages.

Remember: a clever joke or an interesting newspaper article, no matter how engaging, will only remain so for a few days. To ensure that environmental print is indeed inviting, teachers must pay attention to whether students are reading it and routinely "refresh" the examples they display in the classroom (Loughlin and Martin 1987). One teacher we know prominently displayed daily newspaper updates on the Winter Olympics near his "science center." When the updates failed to interest his fourth graders, he moved them to a more prominent area of the room. When students still failed to take much of an interest in the articles, he replaced them with a collection of comics from the local newspaper, which his students found much more inviting.

Classroom traffic patterns also influence where environmental print should be placed. A brief item from a newspaper posted near the pencil sharpener, a place frequently visited by elementary students, is much more likely to be read—and reread—than a similar item placed behind the teacher's desk, where students rarely go. Environmental print placed at students' eye level is more inviting than print placed above their heads (to them, it will seem targeted to adults) (Loughlin and Martin 1987). A first-grade teacher we know was so taken with this idea that she moved the alphabet from above the blackboard, where it is in many classrooms, to below the blackboard, where her students could actually touch (and trace) the letters.

When Curt Dudley-Marling's (1997) third graders entered the classroom each morning, one of the first things they saw was a chart story that included information about the day of the week, birthdays, special events, sports scores, and what he hoped were amusing anecdotes. Many of his students, including his struggling readers, read this chart as soon as they entered the classroom each morning, even before they

A Classroom Teacher's Guide to Struggling Readers

took off their coat. But again, student interest in this sort of thing rarely goes beyond the initial reading. Other types of environmental print—song lyrics, for example—may continue to attract students' attention for weeks or even months.

The important point here is that creating a print rich classroom is more than simply filling a classroom with various forms of environmental print. An effective, print-filled classroom is rich in environmental print that has been carefully selected to respond to students' needs and interests, strategically placed in the classroom, and routinely refreshed.

Books, More Books, and Still More Books

Although print-rich classrooms contain a wide range of texts, none is more important than books. Reading books, particularly "easy" books at their reading level, is fundamental to children's development as readers—and this is especially important for struggling readers (Allington 2000). There is a strong correlation between the number of books children read and the success they enjoy as readers. Yet struggling readers often spend so much time doing skill work that they have fewer opportunities to read real books than their more able classmates do. This is a kind of self-fulfilling prophecy: the *remedy* for struggling readers, more skills, may create reading problems by denying these same students critical reading experiences. Classrooms that effectively support struggling readers must be filled with books, and students must also be given the time—and support—to read them.

An effective classroom library contains a large number of titles on a wide variety of topics likely to interest the students who inhabit that classroom—but that's only a beginning. Classroom libraries—frequently augmented with books from the school and local public libraries—should offer students a range of genres, including realistic fiction, science fiction, historical fiction, poetry, biography, fantasy, folktales, and mysteries.

Different genres have different text structures. Learning to read realistic fiction, for example, involves learning how setting, characters, and plot work together to convey the meaning of the story. In general, children learn to read the various genres by reading those genres. A steady diet of realistic fiction, though important, is insufficient preparation for reading nonfiction, for example. To learn to use the established structures of nonfiction texts—or any other genre—students need experience reading those texts, usually with the active support and direction of their teachers. Therefore, students must have easy access to texts representing a range of genres.

To be considerate of the needs of struggling readers, classroom libraries need to include both challenging and not-so-challenging texts. Struggling readers benefit from a diet of "easy" books at their reading level, but with appropriate teacher support, they also benefit from tackling more challenging texts (Dudley-Marling 1997; Szymusiak and Sibberson 2001). Classroom libraries for young readers often include books in attractive formats: big books, pop-up books, peek-a-boo and accordion books, "touch and feel" books, picture books, multimedia products, and so on.

Regardless of genre, topic, or text difficulty, books that were written to be read are far better than books that were written to teach reading. Decodable texts, sometimes called "linguistic readers" ("the fat cat sat on the hat," for example), fail to teach students how to orchestrate phonetic, linguistic, and semantic cues to construct meaning while reading connected text. A more serious failing, decodable texts obscure the fundamental insight of learning to read: that reading should make sense. So-called "high interest, low vocabulary" versions of books, rewritten to make them more "readable" for struggling readers by stripping away the rich language originally employed, often fail to engage young readers' interest.

Predictable books are an attractive alternative to both decodable texts and high interest, low vocabulary books. Predictable text structures, achieved through the use of rhyme, repetition, cumulative patterns, and familiar story lines (Rhodes and Dudley-Marling 1996), make predictable books relatively accessible to less skilled readers while still encouraging these students to use a range of textual and phonetic cues. Predictable texts also increase the number of words children can recognize on sight.

However varied, classroom libraries must reflect students' interests and their cultural and linguistic backgrounds. Ultimately, teachers must push their students to read widely, but struggling readers are often reluctant readers. Therefore, teachers of struggling readers need to give particular attention to their interests. Talking with students about their interests and keeping track of students' choices of reading material will help teachers ensure that their classroom libraries include authors, topics, and genres most likely to engage their students. Failure to take account of students' interests and their cultural and social backgrounds will likely contribute to the alienation that frequently plagues struggling readers. Recent research indicates that the literacy curriculum in many classrooms does not reflect the interests of boys (see Newkirk 2002, for example), who, as a group, lag behind their female classmates in reading achievement (National Center for Educational Statistics 2003).

Accumulating books for a classroom library—and we've seen classroom libraries that included over a thousand books—can be costly and may take years. There are, however, alternatives to buying new, expensive hardbound books. When we were classroom teachers, we purchased hundreds of books at garage sales and book fairs, and supplemented them with books checked out of public and school libraries. We also included student- and teacher-produced books in our classroom libraries. Some teachers pool their books to increase the range of texts available to their students. Recent basal anthologies, many of which now include excellent selections of high-quality children's literature, can also be used to good advantage (see Chapter 7).

Organizing Your Classroom Library

The physical arrangement of classroom space affects the ease with which students use print resources as well as where and how they read.

Books displayed prominently throughout the classroom—on bookshelves, chalk trays, cabinets, etc.—are more likely to attract students' interest than books stored in a remote corner. Students also find books displayed with their covers facing out more inviting than books displayed with only their spines visible. In our classrooms, we regularly rotated books in prominent locations so that students could more easily see the attractive (and inviting) cover illustrations. And, if we did a unit on folktales or poetry, we made a special effort to display these books with their covers fully visible. Other teachers we know organize their books in bins (by genre). Still others add color-coded labels to book spines to identify genres (blue for fiction, red for mysteries, green for nonfiction, and so on).

A carpeted reading center with comfortable pillows and chairs invites students to read quietly. Round tables, clusters of desks, and open carpeted areas make it more likely students will meet in groups to talk about what they are reading. In Curt Dudley-Marling's third-grade classroom, for example, a group of students who met on the carpet to look through a stack of "scary" books spontaneously created the Scary, Evil Book Club, which met daily to read, discuss, and write scary stories over a period of six weeks (Dudley-Marling 1997). Accessible, comfortable meeting spaces also support teacher-facilitated small-group work.

How a space is organized affects how human beings feel about themselves and their work and how they work together. This is just as true of children as adults. In the end, teachers must routinely evaluate how they and their students use classroom space to determine whether the organization of their classrooms supports their goals for literacy learning. If, for example, students rarely interact around books, preferring to read on their own instead, teachers may want to consider whether the way the classroom is arranged encourages this isolation. Similarly, if teachers find that student disruptions frequently interfere with their individual and small-group work, they may wish to consider reorganizing the classroom to create more private areas. In the end, space matters.

Structures and Strategies for Effective Instruction

Reading Aloud and Minilessons

3

Careful organization of classroom structures and strategies is the key to addressing the individual needs of readers, whether struggling or able. Reading workshop provides room in which to address diverse learning needs within the classroom community, rather than separating struggling students from that community by pulling them out for remedial instruction. It is also an alternative to whole-class instruction, which is rarely effective for struggling readers. Although reading workshop isn't the only way to organize instruction in support of struggling readers, it has worked for us and for many other teachers over the years.

Reading Aloud

The stories our teachers read to us in class when we were children are among our fondest memories. Unfortunately, many elementary teachers are abandoning the practice of reading regularly to their students as they feel the pressure to concentrate on the reading "skills" that are the focus of high-stakes reading tests (Edmondson and Shannon 2002). In the climate of No Child Left Behind, in which reading instruction needs to be justified by appropriate "scientific research," it is easy to see why many teachers may find it difficult to defend a practice that on the face of it appears to be little more than entertainment. Rarely is read-aloud or story time considered instructional time (Hoffman, Roser, and Battle 1993).

Reading fine literature is certainly entertaining, but it also demonstrates the power, purposes, and patterns of written language to students. Teachers who read quality children's literature to their students expose them to a range of genres and authors while broadening students' life experiences. To the degree that they are engaged by books and stories their teachers read to them, it is hoped that students will take up the invitation to read on their own. In addition to these general benefits, research has demonstrated that reading to students positively affects students' reading vocabularies, reading comprehension, reading interests, critical thinking, and the quality of their oral language (Clarke et al. 1995; Hoffman, Roser, and Battle 1993; Huck 1979; McCormick 1977). Clearly, reading quality literature aloud to students is a justifiable instructional activity.

Hoffman, Roser, and Battle (1993) offer teachers the following advice on reading to their students:

- Create a regular time and place for reading aloud to students. (We recommend that reading aloud signal the beginning of the reading workshop.)
- Allow twenty minutes or longer for a scheduled read-aloud.
- Choose high-quality children's literature. This is most likely to engage students.
- Help students make text-to-text connections—to other books by the same authors or to books on similar themes, for example.
- Encourage lively discussions. (Reading to students in smaller groups may spark discussion more easily.)
- Reread selected pieces. This increases the quantity and quality of children's comments while promoting deeper understanding of stories. Let students suggest stories to be reread.
- Value personal responses.

To these suggestions we add some of our own:

- Practice reading aloud, and develop and refine your skill. We've all heard dramatic, engaging, entertaining read-alouds. Teachers should strive to make their oral readings as appealing as possible. Rehearse, especially if the text is unfamiliar.
- Maintain regular eye contact with students while reading.

- Pause before turning the page of a picture book to increase antic-ipation. Leave listeners "ready for more" by not reading too much of a chapter book at one sitting.
- Read to young elementary students several times a day—first thing in the morning, after lunch, just before dismissal. Even if there are just a few minutes between activities, it is possible to read a short poem or essay to students.
- Include a wide range of genres—fiction, nonfiction, folktales, mysteries, poetry, and so on.
- Integrate multicultural literature. Even if you teach in a school with little apparent cultural diversity, find ways to share culturally diverse literature with your students. In a society in which many Americans have few opportunities to interact with people whose life experi-ences are different from their own, multicultural books challenge students to understand and explore unfamiliar perspectives.
- Don't follow every read-aloud with discussion. Not every piece needs to be discussed. Many times, a follow-up activity might be better framed as a minilesson.
- Offer students opportunities to share spontaneous comments.
- Thoughtfully plan postreading discussions so that students develop the highest levels of literate behavior. These discussions need to go well beyond word recognition and rote recall of story lines or textual information.

Minilessons

Minilessons are brief—usually between five and ten minutes—whole-class lessons that address a reading skill or some aspect of reading work-shop. JoAnn Hindley (1998) identifies three types of minilessons that she uses in her classroom: lessons on workshop management; lessons on reading strategies; and lessons on literary elements.

Workshop Management Minilessons

These minilessons address workshop procedures and routines: famil-iarizing students with the physical arrangement of the classroom (where books and other reading materials are stored, preferred places for silent reading, where to keep books from one day to the next); introducing (or reviewing) workshop rules (appropriate activities during reading workshop, putting books back in their designated places, when it is okay to talk, when to keep quiet); giving instructions for specific activities (using tapes in the listening center, using the computers, completing reading logs, performing self-assessments); following daily individual schedules; and so on.

For a reading workshop to be successful, students need to know what they should be doing when, where, and with whom. Students need to be able to work on their own productively while the teacher gives explicit support and direction to struggling students individually and in small groups. Therefore, as much time as necessary should be spent teaching students the routines and procedures.

Workshop management minilessons predominate during the first few weeks of school, although occasional "refresher" lessons may be required throughout the year. For example, JoAnn Gillespie introduced her third graders to reading workshop on the first day of school in an extended minilesson during which she first gave the children a tour of their classroom and reviewed her "Expectations for Independent Reading" (see Figure 3.1) before sending them off for an abbreviated, twenty-minute period of independent reading. During this time, Mrs. Gillespie helped students select reading material appropriate to their interests and abilities and monitored the degree to which they understood her expectations, occasionally reconvening the class if she sensed a problem. When she realized that many of her students were having difficulty selecting appropriate books, she began a series of whole-class minilessons on selecting books.

For the first one, Mrs.Gillespie brought in a stack of books that had been sitting on the nightstand next to her bed. She explained to her class that these were books she had set aside to read when she had time.

Figure 3.1   Expectations for Independent Reading

1.   Each student must have a book, magazine, or other reading material.
2.   Students may listen to "books on tape" but are expected to follow along in a copy of the book.
3.   Students must respect other students' rights as readers.

A Classroom Teacher's Guide to Struggling Readers

She then talked about how she picked one book to read, Barbara Kingsolver's *Poisonwood Bible,* and became so engrossed that she couldn't put it down even when her husband called her for dinner. She shared a couple of passages from the *Poisonwood Bible* to illustrate what made the book so appealing. She also told her class that when she finished the *Poisonwood Bible* after less than a week, she quickly picked another book from the stack. But this book had failed to hold her interest and, after several tries, she gave up and tried another book. She said she'd had trouble getting into other books, too, but was often rewarded if she stuck it out a while. She then asked her students to talk about their own experiences with books they had found particularly engaging, books they had started but gave up on, and books they struggled with at first but eventually couldn't put down. After this brief discussion, Mrs. Gillespie worked with her students to make a number of lists: characteristics of books that grabbed and held their interest almost as soon as they picked them up; characteristics of books that failed to engage their interest; and strategies they used to give books a chance.

The next day Mrs. Gillespie asked the students to reflect on the book choices they'd made the previous day. Follow-up lessons focused on trying out books on unfamiliar topics and genres and deciding whether to stick with a book or not.

Over the next several weeks Mrs. Gillespie conducted a number of additional minilessons related to workshop procedures and routines:

- Following the daily schedule for independent reading.
- Using the listening center.
- Putting books back in their designated places.
- Reading with a partner.
- Doing word sorts (an activity students might be asked to do individually or in small groups—see Chapter 6).
- Coping with reading problems (encountering unknown words, not understanding, etc.).
- Keeping a reading log.
- Completing self-assessments.
- Talking about books with classmates.

When some students had difficulty making an efficient and orderly transition from the whole-group minilessons to independent reading, Mrs. Gillespie devoted a minilesson to it. When several students continued to be disruptive, she instituted a new expectation—the first ten minutes of reading workshop was "quiet time." This worked.

As she taught her students the routines and procedures for independent reading, Mrs. Gillespie gradually increased the time they spent reading independently and expanded the supporting activities students undertook during this period (word sorts, book talk groups, etc.). As her students learned to work independently, Mrs. Gillespie spent more of her time working directly with individual students and small groups.

Reading Strategy Minilessons

Strategy lessons focus on what readers do in order to make sense of texts. Which strategies teachers focus on depends on what they believe readers do as they interact with texts—that is, the theory of reading that stands behind their practice.

All readers use visual information—including sound-symbol relationships and words they immediately recognize—as they read. Debates about phonics are really differences of opinion about the degree to which readers, particularly beginning readers, rely on visual information to make sense of texts. A substantial body of reading theory and research indicates that in most situations, readers use visual information in concert with other cues as they read (see Weaver 2002). This is fortuitous, since visual cues are often ambiguous; that is, the regularities of the English sound-symbol system are not that regular. The phonics rules we were taught in school, by themselves, are not particularly reliable. The old saw "when two vowels go walking, the first does the talking," for example, does not account for words like *chief, siege, beige, belief, quip,* or *break.* As it turns out, most phonics "rules" are applicable less than 50 percent of the time (Savage 2004). These difficulties are compounded by regional differences in pronunciation. In the Northeast, where we live, many speakers say *Hah-vud,* not *Harvard,* and in some parts of the United States *creek* is pronounced *crick.* In other parts of the country, speakers may not distinguish between the pronunciation of *pin* and *pen.* But when readers draw on their knowledge of phonics in concert with other cues, they easily overcome these ambiguities. In the context of connected text, few readers confuse *pen* and *pin* (*she pricked herself with a* pin, *she wrote with a* pen) or conclude that *break* (*when she hit the ground she felt her leg* break) is pronounced with a long $\bar{e}$ sound. And if they did, that would signify less a problem with phonics than an overreliance on sound-symbol relationships to the exclusion of other contextual or linguistic cues.

Cues in addition to phonics and other word-analysis strategies that readers use to make sense of words in connected text include:

- Their knowledge of the grammatical structures of English (syntax).
- Their schemas of how the world works (for example, people are capable of intentional actions, animals and inanimate objects are not).
- Their knowledge of characteristic text structures for various genres (narrative fiction, folk- and fairy tales, mysteries, nonfiction, poetry, and so on).
- Their knowledge of conventions governing the use of language in various social contexts (choices of style, topic, word choice, degree of politeness, and so on) and how the context affects meaning (irony, for example, can only be detected with reference to the social context).

So when a young reader encounters the sentence "The boy ate dinner at a *restaurant* last night," she would likely combine her knowledge of the world (places where people eat), her knowledge of English grammar (the word at the end of a prepositional phrase is likely a noun), and some of the visual cues (our pronunciation of *restaurant,* which is, approximately, *rĕs-ter-ŏnt,* is not entirely predictable using phonetic rules). And if she initially predicted that *restaurant* was pronounced *rē-stor-ĕnt,* she might recognize that this didn't make sense (people don't eat at *rē-stor-ĕnts*) and attempt to repair her error, or *miscue.* Similarly, a struggling reader who confuses *saw* for *was* in the sentence "The boy was going to the store" fails to draw on his knowledge of English syntax as he reads (although he might go on to demonstrate this knowledge by correcting his mistake).

Readers also use a variety of intentional strategies in order to construct meaning from text and deal with problems they encounter in doing so. They question, synthesize, and infer (Keene and Zimmerman 1997). They deliberately relate what they are reading to other texts as well as to their own experiences and background knowledge. They focus their attention on what they believe to be the most important information, usually giving less attention to extraneous details. Depending on their purpose, readers may skim portions of texts they deem less important. Or they may scan the text before they read it in order to get a preliminary idea of the content and structure. Readers will likely adjust their reading rate to the difficulty of the material they are reading. Some readers construct visual images as a means of comprehending texts. Competent readers also monitor their comprehension by routinely asking themselves, *does this make sense?* If it doesn't, good readers have a range of strategies for repairing breakdowns in meaning, including rereading and reading ahead.

Knowing what readers do in the process of reading gives a focus to ongoing assessment, which, in turn, guides teachers as they attempt to give their students appropriate support and direction that push them toward higher levels of literacy.

There are three general categories of reading strategy minilessons: those in which teachers *model* reading strategies; those that rely more heavily on *student participation and discovery*; and those that focus on *explicit instruction* (Pearson and Gallagher 1983; Rhodes and Dudley-Marling 1996). In practice, any given minilesson is likely to be a combination of all three.

Modeling Reading Strategies

Struggling readers are often oblivious to the processes proficient readers use as they make sense of connected text (Rhodes and Dudley-Marling 1996). Many struggling readers believe, for example, that the principal difference between themselves and proficient readers is that proficient readers possess superior phonics and word recognition skills.

As Charles Webb listened to his fourth graders read and discuss books in their literature-sharing groups and his routine reading conferences, he noted a problem. Most of his students were relatively fluent readers who had fairly good recall of what they read. Yet few engaged with these texts at deeper levels, actively relating what they were reading to their life experiences, their background knowledge, or other texts they had read. He decided to show his students how he engaged with the books he read by modeling a think-aloud strategy (Baumann, Jones, and Siefert-Kessell 1993).

Mr. Webb brought a book he was currently reading—*No Heroes,* by Chris Offutt (2002)—to class and began by reading aloud from the book, starting with a page he had identified the previous evening as particularly appropriate for a minilesson on engaging with texts more deeply:

The realtor and I spent a few minutes asking each other about our families. I told him about the house and wrote a check for earnest money. The realtor was surprised that I could buy a house without stepping inside. He said that his wife would never let him do that. I told him we had rented our last four houses over the phone. . . . He shook his head in an incredulous fashion. He'd lived all his life in Morehead, worked in the family business, and was engaged in politics. As a child I had envied the privilege of his family, and now he envied my travels. (32–33)

Here Mr. Webb paused and talked briefly about the many places he had lived and how he often envied people like the realtor who had lived in one place for their whole lives and probably had many friends they had known since they were children. He told his students he had moved so often that it was hard for him to keep track of old friends. Then he continued reading:

> I stepped outside and spoke briefly to a man I remembered from high school. I vaguely recalled something bad about him, but I could not trust the memory because Morehead thrived on innuendo, scuttlebutt, and outright lies. When I was a kid Rowan County had telephone party lines that included two to eight families. (33)

Pausing again, Mr. Webb explained what party lines were. He said his family had had a party line when he was a boy. His neighbors would sometimes listen in while he talked to his high school girlfriend; one neighbor frequently interrupted his conversations, insisting that he give up the line so she could make a phone call even if he'd been talking for only a few minutes. Skipping ahead to a later chapter, Mr. Webb continued reading:

> The other day a man in the video store reminded me that we knew each other thirty years ago. His name was engraved on a small oval of polished brass attached to his belt near the buckle. The last time I saw Jimmy Joe his hair hung past his shoulders. He played guitar in the county's only rock band, drove a red GTO, and had girlfriends galore. (139)

Mr. Webb looked up and noted how many quirky characters Chris Offutt featured in his book. Mr. Webb told his students a bit about Chris Offutt's first memoir, *The Same River Twice* (1993), which included some of the same characters. He also told his class about another of his favorite authors, Anne Tyler, whose books are filled with quirky characters. Then he shared several titles of books in their classroom library that featured odd but funny characters: *Wilfrid Gordon McDonald Partridge* (Fox

1989), *James and the Giant Peach* (Dahl 2000), and *Maniac Magee* (Spinelli 1990).

When Michelle Baker listened to her first graders read aloud, she found that many of her struggling readers read letter-by-letter, word-by-word, and seemed unconcerned about miscues that drastically changed the meaning of the text and sometimes didn't make any sense at all (e.g., "The third little pig made a house out of *drinks*"). So Ms. Baker decided to present a minilesson on strategies her students could use to monitor their comprehension and repair breakdowns in meaning. She began by modeling the simple strategy of rereading parts of the text when meaning is disrupted. She picked up *Strega Nona* (de Paola 1975), which she had read to her class the previous week, and read, "Big Anthony grabbed a cover and put it on the pot and sat on it" (17). "This is what is says in the book," she told the class. "But when I read the story at home the night before I read it to you, I thought it said, 'Big Anthony grabbed a cover and put it on and sat on it.' So I was a bit confused. You can't put on a cover and then sit on it. This didn't make any sense. So I went back and read the sentence again. I saw right away that I had skipped the words *the pot*, and then it made sense to me." Ms. Baker reassured her class that even the best readers often made mistakes like this and that when it happened to them, they might think about rereading a bit of the text to see if they'd made a mistake.

Participating In and Discovering Reading Strategies

In this type of minilesson, teachers and students work together to identify and discuss strategies proficient readers use to make sense of texts. These lessons may be used in conjunction with or independent of teacher modeling.

Mrs. Hancock, a second-grade teacher, discovered a common problem early in the school year. When her struggling readers came to a word they didn't know, they tended to use only one strategy—they attempted to sound the unknown word out. For example, when Lilian encountered the word *throw* in a sentence that began "I throw the stick," she tried to sound out *throw* ("thr-, thr-, thr-") for a full minute before Mrs. Hancock finally gave her the word. Sometimes Lilian was able to sound out unknown words successfully, but more often she was frustrated by a system that didn't work very well for her. Lilian didn't seem to respond to Mrs. Hancock's encouragement to use other cues in combination with "sounding out." In a *reading interview* (see Chapter 4), Lilian shared her conviction that good readers rarely encountered "words they didn't know" but that if they did, they would "sound them out."

Mrs. Hancock decided a whole-class minilesson might help struggling readers like Lilian discover the range of cues good readers use to deal with unfamiliar words. She began by asking her class a simple question: "What do you do when you're reading and come to a word you don't know?" Several students said they would sound it out, but a couple of the most able readers suggested alternatives. One said, "I kind of guess what would make sense." The second volunteered, "I just keep reading and then usually I can figure it out. Sometimes I just go back and read [the text] over again to see if that helps." Mrs. Hancock emphasized that these were reading strategies that she used herself. She recorded the strategies her students had shared on a flipchart, which she then posted on one of the classroom walls for students to refer to when they came to words they didn't know.

Ms. Krall introduced the think-aloud strategy by first modeling it during several minilessons. She then presented a minilesson that encouraged her fifth graders to use the think-aloud strategy with her support. She invited the class to share what they were thinking as she read *Faithful Elephants* (Tsuchiya 1988), a powerful picture book that describes the tragic fate of the elephants at the Tokyo Zoo during the Second World War. Ms. Krall was certain that this book would provoke strong feelings in her students, and it did.

Ms. Krall read, "Two elephants are outside performing their tricks for a lively audience. While blowing toy trumpets with their long trunks, the elephants walk along large wooden logs" (4). Pausing, she asked the students to share what they had been thinking about as she read this page. A number of students talked about trips to the zoo with their families. One student said that once when she visited the zoo she got to ride on one of the elephants. A couple of students talked about going to the circus and seeing elephants do tricks.

As Ms. Krall continued to read, her students learned that this was a story set in the Tokyo Zoo during the awful days toward the end of World War II. "What would happen if bombs hit the zoo?" she read, "If the cages were broken and dangerous animals escaped to run wild through the city, it would be terrible! Therefore, by command of the Army, all of the lions, tigers, leopards, bears, and big snakes were poisoned to death" (8).

Again, Ms. Krall stopped reading and asked her students what they were thinking. For a moment, shocked by what they had heard, they sat in stunned silence. But soon one hand went up, then another. Students mostly talked about how angry and upset they were, but one student was able to acknowledge that the zoo officials probably made the only decision they could have, since "these animals were very dangerous." A couple of students talked about how badly they had felt when their pets died. Then Ms. Krall pushed the discussion beyond personal responses by asking, "Does this story remind you of anything else we've read this year?" One girl, a struggling reader, recalled the story *Baseball Saved Us* (Mochizuki 1995), which was "also about some of the bad things that happened during the war." This led to a far-reaching discussion about war, including some comments from students about the war in Iraq. Ms. Krall concluded this lesson by telling her students that good readers routinely relate what they're reading to their own lives and to other books they've read. She urged her students to do the same while they were reading.

Most of Mr. Parker's second graders were reading connected text independently, but many got confused when they encountered words ending in *gh*. He decided to use participation and discovery to help his students understand the various ways the /f/ sound is represented in English writing. He began by asking them to make a list of words that end in /f/, as in *off*. As his students suggested words like *puff, laugh, stuff, graph,* and *beef,* Mr. Parker wrote the words on a flipchart, sometimes asking if they knew how to spell a particular word. When the list was complete, Mr. Parker challenged his students to identify all the ways the final /f/ sound was represented, and they easily did so: *f, ff, ph,* and *gh*. Mr. Parker then made four columns on the flipchart, and he and his students sorted the words they had generated into the appropriate columns:

–f	–ff	–ph	–gh
deaf	off	photograph	laugh
leaf	puff	telegraph	rough
reef	huff	graph	tough
beef	handcuff	phonograph	trough
wolf	buff	triumph	cough
barf	stuff		
ref	cuff		
chief			
chef			

A Classroom Teacher's Guide to Struggling Readers

He concluded the minilesson by taping the chart on the wall and urging his students to add to the list whenever they came across other words ending with /f/. (A follow-up minilesson focused on various ways English spellings represent the beginning /f/ sound.)

Explicit Minilessons

Explicit instruction also plays an important role in teaching reading. Mr. Hawkins, a second-grade teacher, conducted a brief minilesson, largely for the benefit of his struggling readers, in which he explicitly taught his students how consonant doubling marked vowels as short. Over several days, he extended this lesson by encouraging his students to discern the pattern in the words *stating, patting, caning, canning, voting,* and *rotten,* which they were able to do. When he was confident his students had mastered this pattern he did a similar series of minilessons on the silent *e,* which marks vowels as long.

Literary Element Minilessons

The daily goal for teachers of reading is to push every child in their classroom, including their struggling readers, as far as they can go as readers. The ultimate goal is to teach students to engage deeply and critically with a variety of texts across a range of genres. Toward this end, students must understand literary elements associated with various genres (IRA/NCTE 1996). As articulated by the Massachusetts Department of Education (2001), students become better readers by

> understanding both the structure and the conventions of different genres. A student who knows the formal qualities of a genre is able to anticipate how the text will evolve, appreciate the nuances that make a given text unique, and rely on this knowledge to make a deeper and subtler interpretation of the meaning of the text.

Teachers shouldn't hold back from teaching their students about genre. Knowledge of text structure is among the cues good readers use to make sense of texts. Here in Massachusetts, for example, students are expected to learn about the characteristics of different genres as early as kindergarten. The Massachusetts Department of Education's *English Language Arts Curriculum Framework* (2001) includes the following expectations for nonfiction for students prekindergarten through sixth grade (most states have similar expectations):

- Identify and use knowledge of common textual features (title, headings, captions, key words, table of contents). [pre-K–Grade 2]
- Identify and use knowledge of common graphic features (illustrations, type size). [pre-K–Grade 2]
- Make predictions about the content of a text using prior knowledge and text and graphic features. [pre-K–Grade 2]
- Identify and use knowledge of common textual features (paragraphs, topic sentences, concluding sentences, glossary). [Grades 3–4]
- Identify and use knowledge of common graphic features (charts, maps, diagrams, illustrations). [Grades 3–4]
- Identify and use knowledge of common organizational structures (chronological order, logical order, cause and effect, classification schemas). [Grades 5–6]

A particular problem for many struggling readers, using graphic features of nonfiction texts, was the focus of a minilesson by Mrs. Hampton, a fourth-grade teacher whose class included a significant number of struggling readers. Mrs. Hampton observed that many of her students were failing to attend to maps and timelines in their social studies text, so she presented a series of minilessons to help her students learn how to interpret graphic features in nonfiction texts. She began by modeling a timeline for her own biography. She told her students she wanted them to learn more about her and directed them to the blackboard, on which she had written a few key events in her life: being born; entering first grade; graduating from high school; graduating from college; getting her first teaching job; getting married; giving birth to her children; attending her son's high school graduation; coming in second in a race she spent months training for; and experiencing the death of her father. Adding dates to these events, she showed her students how she could represent these significant events in her life on a timeline.

The next day Mrs. Hampton conducted a follow-up lesson in which she helped two student volunteers create a timeline for significant events in their lives. She then invited all of her students to develop similar timelines for their lives. On the third day, she used an overhead projector to display a photocopy of a timeline from their social studies text depicting important developments in colonial America. She discussed how timelines help readers develop a chronology of historical events.

A Classroom Teacher's Guide to Struggling Readers

Over the next several weeks, Mrs. Hampton used similar lessons to teach her students how to take advantage of diagrams, maps, and illustrations in the social studies textbook.

Ms. Davis used a minilesson to introduce her second graders to an extended unit on folktales. Her goals for the unit included using folktales to introduce the concepts of character, plot, and setting in fiction. On consecutive days, Ms. Davis read two different versions of the story of the three little pigs, a traditional version and *The True Story of the Three Little Pigs,* by Jon Scieszka (1996). After reading the Scieszka version, Ms. Davis asked how the two versions differed and how they were the same. As her students talked, Ms. Davis made two columns on chart paper and recorded student comments:

Two Stories of the Three Little Pigs

How they are the same	How they are different
There's a wolf in both stories.	In the first story there are men who sell the pigs bricks, sticks, and straw.
In both stories, the wolf kills two pigs.	The pigs' mother is in the first story.
The pig in the brick house doesn't die.	The wolf dies in the second story.
Both stories start "once upon a time."	The wolf in the second story is funny. In the first story, the wolf is mean.
In both stories one pig lives in a straw house, one lives in a stick house, and one lives in a brick house.	In the first story, the third pig outsmarts the wolf.

Once the students finished talking about these similarities and differences, Ms. Davis introduced the terms *character* and *plot,* writing them next to the appropriate entries on the chart as she summarized their discussion.

Over the next six weeks, Ms. Davis continued to draw her students' attention to the characteristic structure of folktales. In her very last folktale lesson, Ms. Davis returned to the two versions of the three little pigs story to introduce the literary concept of point of view. She asked her students to reconsider their original list of similarities and differences between the two versions, and one of Ms. Davis's struggling readers observed that the Jon Scieszka version "told the story the wolf wanted you to believe."

Paying attention to literary elements includes helping students appreciate how an author's literary style—word choice, sentence structure, imagery, among other things—contributes to a piece of literature's overall effect. Reading, writing, speaking, and thinking are inseparable. Through a series of minilessons on imagery, Ms. Davis wanted to help her students understand how authors use language to convey images important to the story. She also wanted them to pay attention to images conveyed in a book's artwork and to create their own artwork and writing that conveyed emotions and messages through imagery.

To find texts that lent themselves to this type of activity she consulted the school librarian, who suggested several classic and contemporary books: *Where the Wild Things Are* (Sendak 1988), *The Recess Queen* (O'Neill 2002), *Encounter* (Yolen 1992), and *Owl Moon* (Yolen 1987).

Ms. Davis decided to begin with a minilesson using *Where the Wild Things Are*. She taped over the written text in her copy of the book before asking a member of the class to volunteer to help her read it aloud. Not unexpectedly, the student was surprised—and puzzled—when she realized that the text wasn't visible. Ms. Davis challenged the student and the class to consider how they could "tell the story" without referring to the print. Susan, the student who had volunteered, "read" the story by describing the action depicted in the illustrations.

Together Ms. Davis and the class examined how the artist (in this case also the author) conveyed the meaning of the book through images. The students noticed the characters' facial expressions and the placement of Max, the main character, on the page where he is opposite the "wild things." One student commented how the artist had drawn different body positions for Max showing him controlling the wild things. Another student noticed the size difference between Max and the wild things, commenting, "He must feel pretty good being able to be in charge of creatures so much bigger than he is!" Another student noticed that Max was often drawn up in the air (running down the stairs, swinging in the trees), not always on the ground: "This shows action and fun."

Then Ms. Davis uncovered and read the text and afterward asked the students whether the words the author used added to the messages they had already discussed. Bryant noted that he liked the words "roared their terrible roars and gnashed their terrible teeth" (he acted out the dance of the wild things while he chanted them!). Ms. Davis pointed out that the author repeated these words over and over, adding, "Those words almost let me hear the monsters up close."

On a subsequent day, Ms. Davis presented a minilesson using *The Recess Queen*. This time she didn't cover up the text but read the book once and then returned to each page, asking her students to notice how the illustrator matched the picture to what the author was trying to say with words. The students noticed that this artist made the main character small when she was feeling out of the group but larger when she stood up to a bully. Students also noticed that how the other characters were placed around the main characters depicted fear or support. Ms. Davis reached into a nearby pile of books and showed pictures from several other books in which illustrators emphasized aspects of a character or situation to stress a particular focus or blended colors and textures to show rapid movement or dreaminess. She then asked her students to be illustrators themselves and draw a picture that "sent a message." When students had completed their pictures, Ms. Davis pinned them up in the classroom and encouraged students to talk about the messages their pictures attempted to convey.

Over the course of the week, Ms. Davis continued to share books in additional minilessons. She read *Encounter* and shared her two favorite pages, in which the author uses a simile and repetition to accompany a powerful picture. One page shows an explorer who landed in the Caribbean as a member of Columbus's crew. The protagonist, a Taino boy, describes the explorer's greed for gold: "I leaned forward and stared into their chief's eyes. They were blue and gray like the shifting sea." In another picture the boy jumps ship to escape capture. "Silently, I let myself over the side of the great canoe. I fell down and down and down into the cold water."

Finally, Ms Davis shared a chart that contained text from the first page of *Owl Moon*. She asked her class to follow along as she read:

> It was late one winter night, long past my bedtime, when Pa and I went owling. There was no wind. The trees stood still as giant statues. And the moon was so bright the sky seemed to shine. Somewhere behind us a train whistle blew, long and low, like a sad, sad song.

Then, at Ms. Davis's urging, the students talked about the feelings these words provoked in them, underlining words that were particularly evocative.

After reading the book in its entirety to her class, Ms. Davis handed out pages copied from the book to pairs of students. She asked them to underline examples of words that created images, share these images with other pairs of students, and hang their pages next to the artwork they had created earlier in the week. She ended by encouraging her students to find additional examples of imagery in their independent reading the next week.

Minilesson Wrap-Up

To be effective, *minilessons must emerge from teachers' careful, ongoing assessment of their students* with reference to state, local, and national language arts standards (e.g., IRA/NCTE standards). Some minilessons may address a problem common to a number of their students (e.g., Mrs. Hampton's students' inability to read graphic features of expository texts). Other minilessons should address skills and strategies teachers have determined can push their students, even their most able readers, to higher levels of literacy. (Typically, minilessons are reinforced through individual and small-group work during independent reading.) Whatever the nature of the minilesson, whether it's a one-shot lesson addressing some specific concern or one of a series directed to a wider, more general concept, they need to be planned very carefully and fit into the broader literacy program.

Here are some additional examples of minilessons that can be used to good effect with struggling readers:

If students ...	Minilessons might ...
Struggle with the notions of characters and/or setting	Address these elements through the use of visualization (see Keene and Zimmerman 1997)
Do not make effective | use of contextual cues when reading	Encourage students to predict words in a text, perhaps using overheads or big books

A Classroom Teacher's Guide to Struggling Readers

Have difficulty dealing with "problems" that emerge during reading	Show students how to use sticky notes to mark places in the text where they had difficulty for later discussion, or help them recognize when they are having difficulty with comprehension
Have difficulty reading dialogue	Use picture books with dialogue, perhaps projecting the dialogue on a screen or chart
Have difficulty reading proper names in text	Model strategies for dealing with proper names (e.g., substituting Mr. S. for Mr. Shostakovich)
Have difficulty retelling stories/identifying what's important	Introduce semantic webs or story maps
Have trouble with words beginning with consonant digraphs (e.g., *ph, sh*)	Generate a list of words beginning with /f/ sound, then sort the words into those beginning with *f* and those beginning *ph*
Have difficulty finding books that interest them	Encourage the class to share strategies they use to find interesting books or other reading materials
Do not use context to help them predict the meaning of unfamiliar words	Introduce the prediction strategy: Find a text that includes words with multiple meanings. Write five or six of these words on the overhead or blackboard and ask students to define them. Ask them to read the text and then define the words again. (A follow-up minilesson might use text that includes some words likely to be unfamiliar.)

Do not draw on background knowledge while reading	Introduce strategies for "activating" background knowledge: reading familiar stories, reading alternative versions of stories, watching film versions of stories, discussing what students think a story will be about, previewing the text (using headings, subheadings, etc.)
Get stuck on an author or genre	Introduce different authors and genres
Struggle with metaphors, puns, and other figurative language	Discuss common idioms like "raining cats and dogs" (Jeff Nathan's book of "PUN-oetry," *Calling All Animals,* provides wonderful opportunities for thinking about words: "When it rains cats and dogs are there poodles, and does this lead to hurricanines?")

Continuous Assessment Makes the Difference

There is no magic bullet when working with struggling readers. No approach, no matter how much research seems to support it, has ever been shown to work with all struggling readers all the time (Duffy and Hoffman 1999). The key to reaching struggling readers successfully is knowledgeable, well-prepared teachers who create structures that enable them to provide *frequent, intensive, explicit, and individualized support and direction.*

Independent reading is the heart of the reading workshop. While reading independently, whether individually or in small groups, students have extended interactions with texts. They have the time and the opportunity to use the skills and strategies they have learned with the support of their teachers. During independent reading, students also engage in activities designed to help them learn skills and strategies for reading a range of texts for a variety of purposes. Teachers need to carefully assess their students' reading development and provide individualized and small-group instruction directed to struggling readers' individual needs. Assessment-based instruction develops students' literacy by taking advantage of what they already know and challenging them to take the next step toward the highest levels of reading achievement.

What Gets Assessed?

Teachers must select assessments that focus on the skills and strategies they believe are crucial to students' reading development in both the short and long terms. Assessments that compare students to one another or some arbitrary standard aren't particularly useful for planning instruction. So determining what gets assessed is the first step in creating meaningful assessment.

What teachers assess is a function of their underlying definition of reading, which, in turn, drives their instruction (Barr et al. 1999). Readers use a range of cues and strategies as they make sense of print. Assessment is a matter of uncovering the cues and strategies students use when they read and determining the degree to which readers are making sense of what they read. Several principles underpin effective assessment:

- Assessment must be linked to instruction. For students who struggle, assessment-based instruction considers the wide range of literacy understandings and practices that students bring to their reading in such a way that "you cannot tell the instructional activities from the assessment activities" (Cooper and Kiger 2001, 4).
- Teachers and students both have a role. Teachers collect and interpret data related to students' reading development from a variety of sources both in and outside the classroom. They also design meaningful literacy activities for their students and then ask key questions like, *What am I learning about this child from her work?* and, *How can instruction challenge this child to new learning?* The answers to these questions become the basis for providing appropriate literacy instruction. Students evaluate and participate in their own learning as part of ongoing group and individual conferences with their teachers.
- Teachers' assessments must consider a wide range of factors, including the school, the student's home, and the community, that affect student learning. Teachers need to assume a "philosophy of abundance" rather than a "philosophy of deficit" when teaching students who struggle with school literacy (Miller 1993). For example, instead of asking, *What is the problem with*

A Classroom Teacher's Guide to Struggling Readers

this child who struggles in my class? the teacher might ask, *In what situations does this student look smart and in what situations does she struggle?*

Meaningful assessment for struggling readers should include:

- Their attitudes toward reading and learning: their confidence in themselves as learners, their willingness to take risks in their learning, the connections they make between their literacy lessons and their lives, their willingness and ability to talk about themselves and others as readers.
- The processes they use to make meaning from texts: graphophonic, syntactic, semantic, and contextual cues; background knowledge; comprehension strategies (predicting, skimming, rereading).
- Their knowledge of authors (who they are and how they work), genres, structures, formats, and literary elements such as character development and foreshadowing (Rhodes and Dudley-Marling 1996).
- The way they choose and use texts: reading texts across the curriculum; understanding how authors organize text for various purposes; reading nonprint sources of information such as graphs, pictures, charts; interacting with texts flexibly according to their purpose and nature.
- Their awareness of various aspects of reading: understanding and being able to articulate strategies for making meaning; using time and space to learn to read (keeping track of and building their stamina for engaging in texts as readers and writers—Calkins et al. 1998); articulating the connections they make in order to arrive at meaning; using and critiquing texts for various purposes.

Types of Assessment

Assessments of students' literacy development include standardized, norm-referenced tests and criterion-referenced tests. Mandated state achievement tests can take either form. More important, teachers use local "benchmarks" and informal inventories to assess their students' reading. They also collect observational data such as anecdotal notes, student-generated assessments, and student work. Teachers must always ask, *What gets assessed? What does the assessment mean, to whom? What is its purpose?*

Ideally, assessments:

- Help teachers meet students where they are and plan the next steps for instruction.
- Help students examine their own learning and share what they are learning with their family, their teachers, and their peers.
- Inform family members about their child's literacy growth, what literacy instruction looks like in the classroom, and how they can become involved in their child's literacy development.
- Inform teachers about students' literacy practices outside school.
- Enable teachers to evaluate how their classroom environment supports students' literacy development (e.g., print resources, environmental print, opportunities for students to read).
- Keep school officials informed about students' progress.
- Satisfy district, state, and federal mandates for ongoing assessment.

Understanding the multiple purposes of various assessments, along with the assumptions behind each purpose, helps teachers connect their assessment to their instruction. Routman (2003) urges teachers to keep these assumptions visible at all times. By observing students as they interact with texts and with other persons within the learning environment, teachers are able to keep in mind the complex factors that contribute to student learning rather than teach to a "label" that ignores students' individual strengths and capabilities.

Assessment is vital to choosing and creating instruction that meets the unique needs of diverse learners in diverse communities. When Pat Paugh taught first grade, she quickly discovered that learning that her students were "below grade level" told her nothing about how struggling readers learned or about their specific instructional needs. Teachers need to collect assessments that inform instruction, not depend on those that categorize or "level" children as learners. In this current high-stakes environment, teachers need to "assess the assessments" to determine their purpose and usefulness for classroom instruction. Let's look at a few of them.

Standardized Tests

Standardized tests are, of course, a reality of school life, but they generally ignore specifics about individual students as learners. Nevertheless, in many schools, especially those in poor communities, state and federal funding and the principal's job security are linked to student performance on standardized tests. In these situations, teachers are under pressure to prepare students to take the tests and achieve "proficient" scores. In many schools, literacy instruction is co-opted by direct test preparation immediately before district and state achievement tests. In others, these tests have become the entire curriculum.

Teachers who promote the notion that literacy is making meaning from various texts include test preparation in their instruction but include it differently. Calkins et al. (1998) argue that if children are used to literacy instruction that emphasizes making meaning through certain methods, there's no need to change those methods when faced with familiarizing students with standardized tests:

> It wouldn't make sense for us to teach children to read poetry or nonfiction through one set of methods and to read standardized reading texts through a radically different set of methods. If all year long we structure our children's time in small reading groups, response groups, on-the-carpet, whole-class discussions about books, and if we teach through demonstration, one-to-one conferring, guided reading, and the like, this means we believe these are the most efficient and effective structures and methods available to us for teaching reading. Why wouldn't we then use these same structures and methods for teaching children to read standardized reading tests? If these are the ways of learning that we and this group of children have learned from and become accustomed to, isn't it only logical that we continue to use these methods? (70–71)

Still, including test prep as a unit of study does allow students to view the genre of testing as one of many literacies that they develop within the academic setting. Explicitly making children aware of this genre and encouraging them to evaluate the purpose and structure of these tests includes our students in the dialogue about testing and is an opportunity to introduce critical literacy into the classroom (Luna et al. 2000).

Portfolios

Assessing students' learning using portfolios is common practice in literacy classrooms organized as a workshop. Portfolios are collections of student work and reflections on that work over time. They can take many forms and are used to link assessment and instruction in a myriad of ways. (Jane Hansen's *When Learners Evaluate,* which stresses close evidence of reading, writing, and oral language development, is an excellent resource.)

In some schools, portfolios are a required part of the assessment program: exemplars are provided and connected to the goals of standards-based instruction, and teams of teachers review each portfolio and rate it according to rubrics developed to align student work with grade-level standards. In less formal situations, portfolios contain samples of student work (in-progress drafts as well as finished products) combined with both teacher and student observations and reflections. In either case, portfolios are a way to acknowledge achievement as well as plan future instructional goals.

There are a number of benefits to using portfolios:

- In choosing items for their literacy portfolio, students have a wonderful opportunity to talk about their learning, thereby increasing their metacognitive awareness of, investment in, and ownership of the learning process.
- The classroom teacher has organized evidence of student learning over time and can use it to gauge students' progress and needs.
- Family members and schools administrators can see evidence of student learning.

Running Records

A running record is commonly used in guided reading groups or conferences to assess readers' strategies for unlocking meaning. The teacher listens to a student read orally from a text, marks miscues and corrections on a blank sheet of paper or on a running record sheet (see Clay 1993), and analyzes the miscues to determine what cueing systems need supporting. Usually the recorder places a check mark for each accurately read word, matching rows of checks to lines of text. The general format for miscues looks like this:

Reader's response	Final response
Actual text	Teacher prompt

An example of recording oral reading and some common running record conventions are provided in Figure 4.1.

A Classroom Teacher's Guide to Struggling Readers

Figure 4.1	Running Record Sample and Conventions	
Reader's action	**Notation**	**Example**
Word read accurately	✔	Reader: He was up the stairs in a flash. Text: He was up the stairs in a flash. Record: ✔✔✔✔✔✔✔
Incorrect response	<u>stars</u> stairs	Reader: He was up the stars in a flash. Text: He was up the stairs in a flash. Record: ✔✔✔✔ <u>stars</u> ✔✔✔ stairs

Reader's action	**Notation**
Several attempts to read a word	<u>fast/fl/flat</u> (one error) or <u>fast/fl/flash</u> (no error) flash flash
Self-corrected error (SC)	fa/fla/SC (no error) flash
No response	----- (one error) flash
Insertion of an extra word	<u>quick</u> (one error) -----
The child unable to proceed and is told the word (T)	-----/_____ (one error) flash / T
The child is unable to proceed and asks for help (A)	-----/__A__/__flash__ (one error) flash / / T
Repetition (R)	←———————————————— He was up the stars / R/ SC (no error) He was up the stairs . . .

Surveys and Interviews

Attitude surveys and reading interviews are important sources of information about students' and their families' awareness of themselves as literate people. Questions in a reading interview might include (Goodman et al. 1987):

1. Make a list of everything you've read today in and outside school. Your list might include books, something on the Internet, signs on the road, anything you can think of.
   a. Why did you read each of these?
   b. Underline what you enjoyed reading the most. Circle what you didn't like reading. Can you tell me the reasons for your choices?
2. Are you a good reader? Why or why not?
3. Can you name other people who are good readers?
   a. What makes them good readers?
   b. What are some of the reasons that they read?
4. When you are reading and you come to a word you don't know, what do you do?
   Do you ever do anything else?
5. Do you think ____ ever comes to something s/he doesn't know? (If yes) What do you think s/he does?
6. If you knew someone was having trouble reading, how would you help that person?
7. What would your teacher do to help that person?

Anecdotes and Notes

Observation—Yetta Goodman (1978) calls it "kidwatching"—is essential for linking assessment to instruction. Children's performance of instructional tasks and their understanding of how those tasks relate to developing academic literacy occur within the interactions of daily instruction. Systematic observation of children at work in the classroom over time provides evidence on which to base further instruction, as well as specific evidence of children's learning that test scores don't always show. Knowing what level book is a good match for a child to read (as evidenced by a Developmental Reading Assessment score, for example) tells nothing about a child's ability to choose appropriate books, his motivation to read certain texts, or the strategies he uses to make meaning from the text.

Figure 4.2   Conference Notes

Student: Gloria (Grade 5)

Date	Title of Book	Text Connections	Extensions and Suggestions
1/4/04	*Wringer*, by Jerry Spinelli	Gloria placed sticky notes next to incidents when Palmer feels "bullied" by his friends . . . this reminded her of some playground incidents	I suggest that Gloria keep track of "bully" examples and tell how Palmer is dealing with this problem for our next meeting; this will help Gloria begin to think about how smaller conflicts lead to the larger "conflict" and "resolution" of the story
1/11/04	*Wringer*, by Jerry Spinelli	Gloria shared her list of problem/solutions around bullying that she found in the story	I have Gloria create a "map" to show the different kinds of bullying she noticed—she could benefit from conversation linking her interest in bullying to her reading—maybe ask her to share what she's found in a literature discussion with friends
1/14/04	*Wringer*, by Jerry Spinelli	Gloria has finished the book; she shared her ideas about the problem encountered by Palmer	I ask Gloria if she is interested in seeing how another story about bullying deals with this problem; I suggest she look in the library for a new book
1/22/04	*The Recess Queen*, by O'Neill	Gloria found a picture book at the library with the same theme—bullying; she read it aloud to me and we compared it to *Wringer*—she found the themes in both books	Gloria enjoys reading and talking one-on-one with me; I ask her to read *Recess Queen* aloud and share two questions about bullying with a peer this week

Observational assessments can take different forms, but if they are to provide accurate and useful information they must be numerous, systematic, and planned. Comparing patterns of student learning over time provides a depth of understanding that lets teachers plan instruction that meets the specific and unique needs of the students in their class. Observations may be as simple as notes jotted down (in diaries, on sticky notes, on index cards, in small notebooks, on clipboards) as teachers circulate through the classroom checking on students at work, or they may be published checklists (like those in Lynne Rhodes's *Literacy Assessment: A Handbook of Instruments* [1993] or Jeff Wilhelm's *Guidelines and Student Handouts for Implementing Read-Aloud Strategies* [2001b]), or they may be teacher-created checklists that are closely aligned with the goals for the current lesson or unit of instruction. Figure 4.2 is an example of a form that a teacher might use to keep track of student conferences on independent reading.

Whatever the method, teachers note how students are participating in various literacy activities and look broadly at students as learners. The observations may focus on strengths and weakness, patterns of behavior within certain interactions, cognitive strategies, motivation, interest, learning style, organizational skills, oral language development, written language development, ability to get help when needed, interactions within student/teacher conferences or student/student conferences. Rhodes and Dudley-Marling (1996) recommend including students in this process; either teachers can ask students to record their own observations about their learning, or teachers can share their observations with students in conferences.

Reading Discussions and Retellings

Sharon Taberski (2000) combines an informal type of retelling with reading "discussions" to assess students' attitudes toward reading and comprehension of texts. The level of complexity changes as students make the transition from emergent to transitional to competent stages of reading:

- As students progress from simple retellings that summarize story plot and characters, teachers look carefully at how they offer their interpretations of more involved texts.
- Student understanding at this level includes summarizing to

A Classroom Teacher's Guide to Struggling Readers

include key points; making connections between the text and other texts, life, and the world (Keene and Zimmerman 1997); supporting their ideas by giving examples from the text; and responding emotionally to the text.

- The discussion may also include the students' ongoing ideas about types of books that appeal to them or why they have difficulty choosing or staying with certain pieces.

Teachers who record this information systematically in easily accessible binders or notebooks have a rich source of information for planning instruction.

Miscue Analysis

Miscue analysis (Goodman et al. 1987) is a means of identifying the processes readers use as they read connected text orally. Good readers use their knowledge of the predictable structures of language, their knowledge of the world, and their knowledge of sound-symbol relationships to make sense of texts. Poor readers overrely on one or more cueing systems often to the exclusion of making sense. When good readers produce miscues that result in nonsense or significantly change the meaning of the text, they tend to correct them. Poor readers do not.

Miscue analysis enables teachers to learn if students are using the range of cues good readers use or if they overrely on certain cueing systems as poor readers do. Students' overall profile of miscues leads directly to instructional strategies. If a struggling reader is overly dependent on decoding, for example, teachers can plan lessons that encourage the student to use other cueing systems (e.g., her knowledge of the world, her knowledge of language) for making sense of texts. Miscue analysis also helps determine the degree to which students are attempting to make sense of text as they read (versus sounding out individual words): good readers always endeavor to make sense. Miscue analysis can also be used to help students select books that they can read independently.

There are a number of versions of miscue analysis. Here we offer a greatly simplified procedure. To begin with, teachers should, in conjunction with the student, select a text that is somewhat challenging and unfamiliar but not frustrating (a frustrating text is one a student reads with less than 90 percent accuracy). It is very helpful to have a copy of the text on which the teacher can make notes. It may also be helpful to audiotape the child's reading of the text for more careful analysis.

In general, miscue analysis involves comparing the text as it appears on the page with the text the student produces. If the student's reading includes miscues, ask the following questions (miscues that do not change the meaning of the text should not be counted):

1. Does the miscue result in text that sounds like conventional language? (*The first little pig made a horse out of straw* sounds like language. *The first little big made a house out of straw* does not.)
2. Does the miscue look or sound like the word in the text? (The substitution of *horse* for *house* looks like the word in the text, as does *big* for *pig*. The substitution of *auto* for *car* does not.)
3. Does the miscue make sense? (*The first little big made a house out of straw* does not make sense.)
4. Does the miscue change the meaning of the text?
5. If the miscue results in a significant change in meaning or, worse, makes no sense, does the student correct the miscue?

Figure 4.3 is a form on which teachers can record and analyze miscues.

Assessment Tools in Action

Let's take a look at some assessments and the strategies for incorporating them in the context of a specific school and a specific teacher. In a large urban school district in our area, multiple assessments of students' literacy learning are used in the early grades. They include a criterion-referenced state achievement test; a norm-referenced standardized achievement test; the Developmental Reading Assessment (DRA) (Beaver 2001); a district phonics survey; the Observation Survey (Clay 1993); and, for older students, a midterm test from the district-adopted basal.

Many of these tests are intended to comply with national and state laws (such as the school report cards mandated by the NCLB

A Classroom Teacher's Guide to Struggling Readers

Figure 4.3	Form for Recording a Modified Miscue Analysis				
Word as it appears in the text	Student's miscue	Does the miscue sound like language?	Does the miscue look or sound like the word in the text?	Does the miscue significantly affect the meaning?	Was the miscue self-corrected?

legislation) and therefore don't relate directly to classroom instruction. Still, these group achievement tests are sometimes used to meet and refine learning goals in the school and classroom. For example, after analyzing the results of the state test item by item, the principal and literacy coordinator in one school noticed that the majority of students were not making universal connections to texts that went beyond their personal experiences. Helping them do so became a schoolwide literacy goal. In addition, since using the DRA as an informal reading inventory twice a year was an insufficient means for identifying needs and planning instruction for struggling readers, the principal asked teachers to complete biweekly running records for those students, and she helped teachers review and analyze them.

Andrea Florence, a teacher who works in this school district, keeps organized records of district-mandated tests for each of her students but also uses other assessments more closely linked to instruction:

- Writing portfolios of in-progress and final-product writing samples, supplemented by three writing prompts a year.
- Running records of students' oral reading in guided reading groups. (She analyzes those of struggling students particularly closely.)
- Surveys and interviews with students and parents, especially parents of struggling students.
- Reader response journals that include a reading log and comments about reading. (Andrea responds in writing, establishing a regular dialogue with her students.)
- Anecdotal and observational notes regarding a variety of literacy events and interactions for each child, especially those who are struggling.
- Well-organized records of all special education meetings, tests, and goals.
- Records of students' writing and reading conferences, to include a list of the strategies students have worked on and are currently working on.

As Andrea uses these assessments, she refines them over time to better meet her needs and the needs of her students.

Recently, Andrea has noticed that Felicia, one of her fourth graders, is struggling with her reading. She reads slowly, word-by-word, and seems more intent on getting through it than making sense of what she reads. Felicia is a hard worker and completes every assignment. However, when asked to retell a story, she supplies a few details but not much else to indicate a meaningful understanding of the text. A conference reveals that Felicia and her mother are working hard on reading at home. Her mother, who herself had a struggle learning to read, urges Felicia to "sound out" every word she encounters. This makes for very uncomfortable and frustrating sessions.

Andrea asks Felicia to fill out a reading attitude survey. She also administers a miscue analysis and takes frequent running records as Felicia reads orally. These assessments indicate that overall Felicia is a moderately proficient reader with an excellent understanding of phonics. However, if she is unable to sound out an unknown word, Felicia reads on, rarely correcting her miscues. Thus, when it comes time to retell the story, Felicia is unable to recall more than a few basic details. Also, Felicia's retelling never includes any personal connections to the story or the characters.

Andrea also keeps observational notes of Felicia's literacy activities in the classroom. For example: "Felicia is so concerned with reading the words exactly as she sees them that she does not focus on what the author is trying to tell the reader." Andrea observed Felicia during a guided reading group early in the year and wrote, "As the story discussion continued, Felicia did what was asked of her, but really did not go beyond that. When instructed to read the story and stop at a particular page, she did just that and then put her head down when done. She did not really practice the goal strategy, pause–think–retell."

Based on her analysis of these assessments, Andrea feels that Felicia needs to focus on comprehension strategies such as looking for context clues when her phonetic knowledge does not help her identify unknown vocabulary and making personal connections (to self, to other texts, and to the world) in her reading. She also decides to incorporate story grammar (see Figure 4.4) and think-alouds into Felicia's instructional plan.

Thinking aloud is a good fit in a classroom in which assessment drives instruction. In this technique, students verbalize their thoughts while reading, thus adding a level of metacognition to their understanding of how they are making sense of the texts they read. Eventually they become aware of strategies for comprehending written text and begin to monitor themselves, either with partners or on

Figure 4.4   Story Grammar

A story grammar, sometimes known as a story map, outlines the basic structural elements of a narrative text. These elements include characters, setting, logical sequence of main events, problem or conflict, and resolution. Mapping a story can be a formal or informal process that includes an oral, artistic, or written response. (A librarian Pat worked with had her students "clap" out the story elements in rhythm—"Characters, setting, plot, and theme"—and then apply these elements to the story they were reading.) Many teachers ask their students to "web" the story in a series of connected boxes or ovals using a computer drawing program such as "Kidspiration" (Inspiration Software Inc.). A simple story map created with that software is shown below.

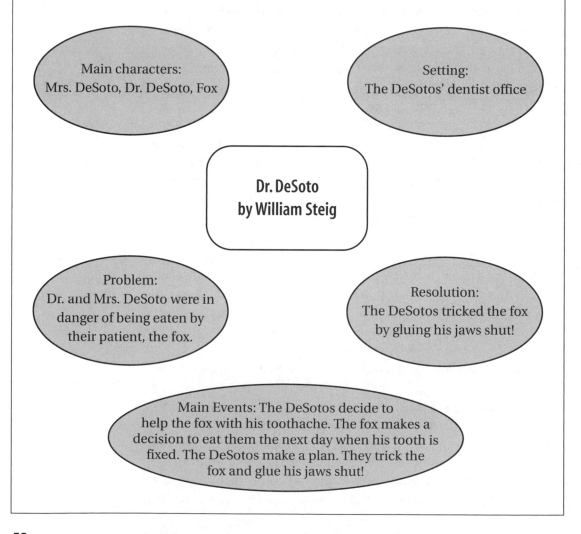

their own. (Jeff Wilhelm [2001a] suggests that teachers and students monitor comprehension strategies such as using personal background knowledge to make connections to text, making and revising predictions, asking questions of the text, visualizing or using imagery, recognizing and solving problems with understanding text, and using "fix up" strategies.) Andrea introduces thinking aloud by modeling her thinking about her own reading in front of her students. She easily incorporates thinking aloud into her reading conferences with Felicia.

In December, Andrea records this observation: "Felicia is reading *There's a Tarantula in My Homework* [Clymer 1999] independently during reading workshop. During a conference, Felicia showed me how she marked the text to share with her partner. She read to me and explained why these parts were funny. Felicia told me that she has reached chapter 4, and she just started the book on Tuesday. She has been reading the story for homework as well." Felicia is beginning to make meaning and also enjoy reading independently.

Based on Felicia's reading interview, a conference with Felicia's mother, and Felicia's low performance on a citywide test, it would seem that Felicia feels she is not a competent reader and that this affects her willingness to invest herself fully in reading and writing activities. Andrea decides that asking her to read to a group of younger special-needs children in a nearby resource classroom will give Felicia an authentic opportunity to interact with and invest herself in texts. Together, Andrea and Felicia choose the picture book *Click, Clack, Moo: Cows That Type* (Cronin 2000). Felicia practices with the book for a week before her first read-aloud, working on her fluency. Andrea helps her pay attention to the dialogue and works with her on how to interpret it expressively. Andrea records the following observation: "The first few times that Felicia went to read to the group, I could see that she was uneasy. She would highlight words that she could not figure out or did not know and then ask me for help. I saw that she was aware of the stories she was reading and of herself as a reader." As the school year continues, Felicia begins to enjoy these sessions and asks to continue them. Andrea writes, "Now, Felicia will choose a book two nights before she has to read it, and tell me about it and why she has chosen it. I am very impressed with Felicia's success; not only is she aware of herself as a reader, but now she is aware of her audience."

Throughout the year, Andrea continues to focus on Felicia's investment in reading and writing as well as on specific strategies Felicia can use to make sense of text. Her ongoing assessments help her set specific instructional goals—spelling accuracy, topic development—during the year. At one point, she takes some writing samples from Felicia's portfolio, shares them with her fellow teachers at a "looking at student work" session, and asks for her colleagues' help in using them to design additional assessments and goals for Felicia.

Andrea uses the template from *Assessing Literacy with the Learning Record: A Handbook for Teachers, Grades K–6* (Barr et al. 1999) to consolidate her assessments and observations. When the year ends, she is able to pass this record on to Felicia's fifth-grade teacher as a complete picture of Felicia's progress and needs.

Individual Support and Direction for Struggling Readers

A reading workshop gives teachers many opportunities to collect detailed assessment data. Informed by this assessment, teachers can address struggling readers' specific learning needs individually and in small groups during independent reading. Small-group work tends to focus on guided reading and literature-sharing groups. Individual work typically takes place in the context of relatively brief (five or ten minutes) reading conferences in which teachers can listen to students read, recommend books (and help them select books appropriate to their interests and reading level), suggest new strategies for reading, offer specific reading instruction, and conduct routine assessment (Taberski 2000).

Individual Support and Direction

All students require some degree of individual support. Struggling readers generally require a higher level of individual support. Let's meet two struggling readers, Melissa and Jacob, as a way of illustrating a range of appropriate strategies for working with struggling readers individually.

Melissa: Reading More Fluently

Melissa is a dysfluent reader. Her oral reading is slow and halting, with little or no expression. Her teacher, Mr. Garcia, has observed that Melissa's oral reading is marked by an overattention to letters and letter sounds. A miscue analysis indicates that when Melissa comes to a word she "doesn't know," she relies heavily on sounding it out. Her miscues tend to look or sound similar to the word in the text (e.g., *fall* for *fill*), but often result in text that is grammatically inappropriate (e.g., *The glass was* falled *with water*), sometimes making little sense. Melissa's responses to a reading interview reinforce Mr. Garcia's conclusion that for Melissa, reading is primarily a matter of sounding out letters and words. Since making sense is not always a priority for Melissa as she reads, her comprehension is generally poor.

Based on this assessment, Mr. Garcia decides that his primary goal for Melissa is to get her to read more quickly and use a wider range of cues as she reads. The instructional strategies he uses over a period of months include:

- *Assisted reading.* To draw Melissa away from the slow, halting style that characterizes her oral reading, Mr. Garcia reads along with her, lowering his voice when her reading is fluent, but raising his voice when she begins to stumble. Mr. Garcia's support helps Melissa read quickly enough to take advantage of contextual cues for dealing with unfamiliar words. In a variation of assisted reading, Mr. Garcia often asks Melissa to read along with audiotaped versions of stories during independent reading.
- *Repeated reading.* Mr. Garcia often asks Melissa to read the same text over several days to increase her fluency and the number of words she recognizes on sight. A reading buddy program with a first-grade class gives Mr. Garcia an authentic reason to encourage Melissa to practice reading a single text—she needs to be able to read it fluently to her first-grade reading buddy. (Mr. Garcia often combines repeated and assisted reading in his work with Melissa.)
- *Responding to her oral reading miscues.* To encourage Melissa to go beyond sounding out unfamiliar words when she reads, Mr. Garcia responds to her oral reading miscues in ways he hopes will encourage her to supplement phonetic cues with contextual cues when she comes to words she doesn't know. For example,

when Melissa's miscues preserve the meaning of the text (e.g., *house* for *home*), Mr. Garcia either ignores the miscue or praises Melissa for her attention to meaning. When Melissa's reading is disrupted by long and unproductive efforts to sound out words, Mr. Garcia encourages her to "read on" to see what word made sense there. When Melissa produces miscues that do not make sense, Mr. Garcia repeats what she has read (e.g., *The first little big made a house out of straw*) and asks if this makes sense (Rhodes and Dudley-Marling 1996).

- *Shared reading.* Shared reading provides "numerous opportunities to show children what reading is all about" (Taberski 2000, 91). While reading a big book with Melissa, Mr. Garcia shows her ways to figure out words:
  - "Look at the first letter."
  - "What makes sense here?"
  - Covering up words with sticky notes and asking her to "guess" the word.
- *Preparing cloze exercises.* Instructional cloze is a fill-in-the-blank exercise that encourages students to make sense using contextual cues. For example, "The dog is chewing on the _____" requires that students make predictions based on their knowledge of syntax (only nouns make sense here) and their knowledge of what dogs typically do (e.g., chew on bones, sticks, or furniture). An alternative construction, "The _____ threw the ball for the dog," requires students to read ahead to determine a response that makes sense, again drawing on their knowledge of syntax (only a noun is appropriate here) and their knowledge of the world (who is capable of throwing a ball?). An alternative to instructional cloze, synonym substitution (Rhodes and Dudley-Marling 1996) asks students to write (or say) another word that makes sense above a word that has been underlined (e.g., "The dog is <u>running</u> in the park").
- Encouraging her to read silently as much as possible.

Jacob: Learning About Phonics

Jacob seems to have figured out that reading ought to make sense, and he tries to create text that is syntactically and semantically appropriate (e.g., *The horse shook his* man [for *mane*]). But his phonics skills are generally weak. As in the *man/mane* example, Jacob is generally unsure of the orthographic cues that mark vowels as long or short. So Jacob's teacher, Mrs. Roach, decides that, in addition to having Jacob participate in a guided reading group, she will create individual lessons for him during independent reading that zero in on phonics skills. The lessons she plans for Jacob include:

- *Shared reading of predictable books* (Cunningham 2000). Mrs. Roach and Jacob routinely read predictable books that emphasize rhyming words. This allows her to emphasize the role of onsets and rimes in decoding. (Onsets are consonants that come before the vowel; rimes are the "obligatory" vowel and any consonant that may come after the vowel—for example, /w/ /ed/, /d/ /og/ [Moustafa 1997].) After Mrs. Roach and Jacob read a book together, they often generate lists of rhyming words that use similar onset-rime schemes (e.g., /t/ /ug/, /b/ /ug/, /h/ /ug/, /l/ /ug/, /m/ /ug/, /j/ /ug/).
- *Teaching common root words* (Cunningham 2000). Throughout the school year, Mrs. Roach schedules lessons with Jacob to draw his attention to root words and affixes. Often these lessons begin with Mrs. Roach giving Jacob a word like *play* and working with him to create as many new words containing *play* as he can (*play*er, *play*ing, re*play, play*ful, *play*house, *play*ground, etc.).
- *Figuring out big words* (Cunningham 2000). Mrs. Roach designs a series of lessons for Jacob on strategies for figuring out "big words." Generally, these lessons focus on chunking words, often by identifying syllables, root words, and affixes. Mrs. Roach often follows up these lessons with individual activities (see Chapter 6) for Jacob to complete, like word sorts.

Working in Small Groups

Teacher-directed small-group work is also a feature of reading workshop. Small groups enable teachers to provide explicit support and direction that addresses the learning needs of several students at once in a social context in which students learn from the teacher and from one another.

A Classroom Teacher's Guide to Struggling Readers

Flexible grouping is the hallmark of group work in the reading workshop. Instead of setting up semipermanent, fixed-ability groups, which are often detrimental to student learning (Dawson 1987; Hiebert 1983), teachers should work with short-term groups of students who have common instructional needs.

Guided Reading

Each day during independent reading, Mr. Coltrane meets with small groups of his third graders for a guided reading lesson. These are flexible groups formed around ongoing assessment.

Recently, Mr. Coltrane's analysis of students' story retellings has indicated that several of his struggling readers are having trouble drawing inferences from what they are reading. These students demonstrate relatively good understanding of the structure of story grammar and grasp surface ideas from stories they read, but more subtle meanings—humor and innuendo, for example—seem to elude them. For example, Parah doesn't mention several details important to the plot of the chapter book she is reading, *The Landry News* (Clements 1999), when she discusses it with Mr. Coltrane. Mr. Coltrane suspects that Parah and several other students are glossing over unknown words and therefore missing the deeper meaning of the text. Full comprehension of written text requires knowledge of the language, knowledge of the world, and knowledge of subject-specific vocabulary. Mr. Coltrane reasons that his students will make the connections required for deeper comprehension if they strengthen their attention to the rich, subject-specific vocabulary contained in the stories they are reading.

Mr. Coltrane decides to use picture books to prompt a deeper attention to interesting vocabulary and how the author uses these words as literary devices. He plans a series of lessons in the context of a guided reading group made up of Parah and several other students, designing activities before reading, during reading, and after reading. He hopes these lessons will also help students learn how to deal with unfamiliar words they encounter in their reading.

Mr. Coltrane selects *Dr. DeSoto*, by William Steig (1990), for his first guided reading lesson with this group, since it can be read in one session and deals with a topic familiar to most students—going to the dentist. It also contains rich, subject-specific vocabulary associated with dentistry.

After Mr. Coltrane and his students assemble at the reading table, he hands each student a copy of the book. To begin the lesson, he encourages each student to "look, talk, share, predict" (Education Department of Western Australia 1994). First, he asks the students to *look* quickly through the book and *predict* what genre, or type of text, it is (fantasy, informational text, etc.), what the plot and theme might be, and what they think the setting and characters are going to be like. When one student comments that the book is about going to the dentist, Mr. Coltrane quickly encourages the group to *talk* about and *share* their own knowledge about and experiences with dentists. Mr. Coltrane then draws his students' attention to a flipchart on which he has written some subject-specific words and phrases related to dentistry that the students will find in *Dr. Desoto*:

rotten bicuspid
drill
gas
extractor
feeling woozy
molded a tooth
socket
permeate the dentine

Mr. Coltrane then asks his students what they already know about these words and, as they talk, he writes their responses on the flipchart. The students know something about most of the words, but they are completely baffled by the phrase *permeate the dentine*.

Mr. Coltrane encourages this group of struggling readers to consider all the ways readers can determine the meaning of a word or phrase they don't recognize as they are reading. The students identify the following resources for coping with unknown words or phrases as they are reading:

- Look the word up in the dictionary.
- Ask classmates or the teacher.
- Refer to the pictures (if it's a picture book).
- Search the Internet.
- Look at the other words in the sentence.
- Match the phrase to similar words.

One student has heard of Dentine, a gum that claims to clean teeth. Based on this information, he thinks that *permeating the dentine* might have something to do with cleaning teeth.

Next Mr. Coltrane asks his students to predict what is going to happen in *Dr. Desoto*. Several students guess that the story is about animals going to the dentist. Before the students read the story silently, Mr. Coltrane urges them to "be on the look out" for interesting or unfamiliar words and phrases as they read. He gives them small sticky notes on which to record these words or phrases.

After they have read the book silently, the students have a lively discussion about the story. Mr. Coltrane wants to know what kind of problems the characters in the story encountered and how they solved them. Parah's friend Jamal offers that the fox definitely had several problems. First, the fox had a toothache, but then he had to decide whether or not to eat the dentist and his wife. Parah interrupts, reminding Jamal that Dr. and Mrs. DeSoto also had a problem: how could they keep from being eaten by the fox? Kara says that the couple's solution of gluing the fox's jaw shut has "really solved both problems." Several students also want to talk about parts of the story that they have found amusing. Jamal says that he thinks the "extractor" fashioned by Dr. and Mrs. DeSoto was "pretty cool."

Other students ask questions about parts of the story that they don't understand. For example, Kara wonders why the dentists let the fox in for treatment in the first place. "They had a sign outside that they wouldn't treat large animals, so they should have known better." When someone suggests that "the mice were brave," Kara responds that they might be brave, but obviously they were not very smart. Mr. Coltrane asks Kara if they seemed smart to her by the end of the story, after they had tricked the fox. "They had to be to make up for their mistake," Kara suggests. Mr. Coltrane asks the group again about their sense of the meaning of *dentine* now that they have read the story. After a brief discussion, the group infers that the glue must have settled into the surface of the fox's tooth.

Students now identify additional words or phrases they have marked with sticky notes. Parah notes that the author uses the word *dainty* to describe the drill used by the dentist, who is a mouse. Mr. Coltrane suggests that they reread the page where *dainty* is used and then challenges them to find any other words that emphasize how small the mouse in the story is. Jimmy immediately suggests the word *delicate*. As the conversation continues, students add more words to their list, noting that some, such as *extractor* and *dentine,* are "dentist words," but others, such as *dainty* and *delicate,* are not. Mr. Coltrane points out how words like *dainty* and *delicate* help him as a reader imagine what it might feel like to be a little mouse inside a large fox's mouth. Kara points to another term, *rotten bicuspid,* and says it helps her imagine the fox's bad breath.

The following day, Mr. Coltrane challenges the four students he's worked with on *Dr. DeSoto,* in pairs, to write their own version of *Dr. DeSoto.* He urges students to add new characters, alter the details, or completely change the ending. In particular, he encourages them to include "interesting vocabulary" in their version. The students work together on this task and then regroup later in the day to share their adaptations. Mr. Coltrane is pleased that this group of struggling students has used some of the subject-specific vocabulary from the original story. One pair of students have also used words like *muffler, wrench,* and *speedometer* in changing their story into one about a mouse who fixes motorcycles.

Over the next several weeks, Mr. Coltrane follows up this lesson during his routine reading conferences with these students.

Literature Sharing

Literature sharing, a regular feature of most reading workshops, provides an opportunity for small groups of students (ideally three, four, or five) to read and discuss common texts with the support and direction of their teacher. Literature-sharing groups are a way for students to engage in literate talk, learn about literary elements (characters, plot, setting, etc.), develop higher levels of reading comprehension, and, above all, experience the pleasure of rich conversation around quality literature.

In the following example, a mixed-ability group, which includes Nicholas, a struggling reader, has read a children's version of Edgar Rice Burrough's *Tarzan.* Here they are discussing Nicholas's assertion that Tarzan's mother was an ape (this transcript is excerpted from Dudley-Marling 1997):

Hugh: His mother wasn't really an ape. He just thinks that because he was *raised* by an ape.

Ali: Yeah, he was raised by an ape. Apes killed his mother.

Paul: Where was his dad?

Hugh: Someone killed him.

[*Students page through the book talking about what happened at various points in the book. One of them points to a picture of Tarzan as a boy.*]

Nicholas: Is Tarzan crying?

Ali: He lost his [*inaudible*] because he didn't know what to do and his father died. And the ape heard the baby crying and the ape was called Caliph.

[*A chorus of no's.*]

Hugh: Geez, man.

Ali: This is his mother [*pointing to a picture of an ape*]. Doesn't this look like his mother?

Hugh: You said the ape was called Caliph.

Ali: The ape was called Caliph.

Hugh: No, it wasn't.

Teacher: Can you show us the part where it says his name is Caliph?

Ali: Yeah!

Hugh: You're nuts. [*Pages through book.*]

Ali: Okay, now I'll prove it. I'll prove it now [*turning pages*]. I'll prove that the ape's name was Caliph.

Scott: What page is it?

Ali: Okay, now, this girl [*pointing to a picture in the text*] was named Alice, right? And this guy, what's his name?

Paul: Jonathon.

Ali: Yeah, John. That's not his mother and father. I'll prove to you that his mother was Caliph, because none of them are named Caliph, and then look at the end.

Ali: [*Reading from the text*] I was born [*inaudible*]. My mother was an ape.

Hugh: His mother wasn't an ape. He just thinks that.

Ali: Caliph. Caliph. Here. There [*pointing to a place in the text*]. That little bit, part. Her [*inaudible*] fallen to death, Caliph had to take a chance. She jumped from one tree to another. The two trees were far apart. Caliph made it, but the baby did not.

Ali: The woman was called Alice, the man was called Jonathon Stokes, and the ape was called Caliph.

Hugh: But back here you said their names are Alice and Jonathon, right?

Ali: Yeah.

Hugh: You said that they weren't the mother and father.

Ali: No, these were the mother and father, but he grew up with Caliph.

In this discussion, students use language as a means of working together to make sense of the story. They challenge one another's interpretations using references to the text to buttress their arguments. Nicholas in particular draws on the support of his classmates to make sense of the story and strengthen his comprehension skills. (Although the teacher is relatively quiet here, he works with the group over the next two weeks to push the group to use the text to support their arguments.)

Literature-sharing groups are a powerful means for engaging students in more complex (and social) readings of texts. Struggling readers like Nicholas may derive particular benefits from this kind of social interaction. Unfortunately, struggling readers often have fewer opportunities to experience the richness of literature sharing with a group of peers. It's especially important that struggling readers regularly participate in literature-sharing groups with appropriate support and direction from their teacher. Mixed-ability groupings like the one above make it easier for struggling readers to participate in literature-sharing groups.

Throughout this text we have emphasized the importance of "frequent, intensive, explicit, and individualized support and direction" for struggling readers. Indeed, all readers require some measure of explicit support and direction. However, explicit support and direction is often missing from literature-sharing groups. Many teachers seem satisfied if students read and discuss books together. Therefore, we want to emphasize the importance of setting clear goals for literature sharing and providing students with the explicit support and direction needed to achieve those goals. In the above transcript, the teacher's goal for this particular group was to encourage students to refer to the text to support their arguments. For other literature-sharing groups the focus may be on making text-to-text connections, focusing on character or setting, making inferences, reading critically, and so on. But there *must* be goals for literature sharing as well as explicit support and direction from the teacher. There is pleasure in coming together to talk about books, but merely talking about books without some sense of where that talk is supposed to lead is insufficient. Teachers must always endeavor to push all their students, including the struggling readers, as far as they can go as readers and provide the necessary support and direction.

6 Self-Directed Learning Activities

S tudents' principal occupation during reading workshop is, of course, reading independently. They need an extended period in which to read texts and use the skills, strategies, and processes their teacher has introduced. We cannot overemphasize the importance of students reading independently.

Designing Independent Learning Activities

In addition to reading independently, most teachers find it useful to design independent activities that strengthen students' use of various reading skills and strategies. Below is a sampling of independent activities useful for struggling readers. Remember, these are *supplemental* activities; they should not take the place of lengthy engagements with books and other texts.

Word Sorts/Word Study

Word sorts encourage students who are still learning how sound-symbol relationships work in reading to analyze words and look for patterns. In general, word sorts require children to look at words—usually written on cards—and sort them into categories based on spelling patterns and sound (Cunningham 2000). Word sorts can also be used as minilessons, if appropriate. Some possible categories for sorting words (from Fountas and Pinnell 1996) include:

- Rhyming words.
- Words with the same initial/final letter or sound.
- Words with the same initial/final letter cluster (*spray/sprite/sprinkle, mast/cast/last*).
- Words with the same vowel sounds (*play/wait/gate, dare/bear*).
- Words with the same number of syllables.
- Word types (grammatical functions) or categories (names, places, food).
- Words with similar letters that have different sounds (*bow/now, she/the/they*)
- Words with different letters but similar sounds (*phone/fine, staff/graph*).
- Words with the same prefixes or suffixes.

Word sorts help students discover word patterns and develop word-analysis skills. Extensive work with words and letters in isolation, however, can distract struggling readers from the fundamental purpose of reading—making sense—and therefore should be avoided (Fountas and Pinnell 1996).

Responding to Text in Writing

Worksheets are common fare in many elementary classrooms, and thoughtfully prepared worksheets can offer students valuable practice with previously taught skills. It is doubtful, however, that a steady diet of worksheets is very helpful, and to the degree that worksheets reduce the amount of time available for reading connected texts, they may be harmful. And some kinds of worksheets ("circle the pictures of words beginning with the /m/ sound") will always be of dubious value. Still, the following kinds of written activities —if used judiciously—can be useful to struggling readers.

Cloze Tasks

Instructional cloze (see Chapter 5), which encourages students to make predictions based on meaning and grammatical structures, can be useful for students who overrely on sound-symbol cues. Cloze exercises ought to respond directly to students' assessed needs. For example, if a miscue analysis or running record indicates that a student effectively uses syntactic and meaning cues up to the point of the miscue but not after (the student reads, "The man put the *tree* around his neck," instead of, "The man put the *tie* around his neck," and doesn't correct the error), then the cloze exercises should encourage that student to use cues after the blank to create meaning ("The ____ bit the man"; "The girl cut her ____ with a saw"). But, again, it is important not to overuse activities like cloze.

Innovations on Text Structures

In innovating, students take a pattern from a familiar text and create their own version. It is effective with students at an early stage of reading development who do not pay sufficient attention to print. For example, instead of "Brown Bear, Brown Bear, what do you see?" (Martin 1970), teachers might help students generate similar alternative text ("Santa Claus, Santa Claus, what do you see?) (Rhodes and Dudley-Marling 1996).

Completing the Story

Students are given a story without an ending and asked to write one. This strategy supports the development of reading comprehension.

Reading Journals

Reading comprehension is not limited to that moment in which readers are visually processing a text. Readers continue to make sense of texts over time as they think about, discuss, and respond in other ways to something they've read. Keeping a reading journal is a way for students to extend their comprehension by engaging more deeply with texts over an extended period. In interactive journals, teachers and students carry on a conversation in writing about a text. For journals to be useful, however, they must be meaningful to students. Contrived prompts (*imagine yourself as one of the characters*) are rarely useful. Students will also benefit from minilessons that model increasingly sophisticated responses to text.

Projects

Author studies and thematic research projects develop critical reading skills; students can undertake them individually or in small groups.

For an author study, students research a favorite author (Jenkins 1999 is an excellent resource on author studies). An author study may include lists of books by the chosen author, book reviews, biographical information, drawings, and so on. Detailed information on authors is easily obtained at a number of Internet sites. The Internet School Library Media Center (ISLMC) (*http://falcon.jmu.edu/~ramseyil/childlit.htm#F*) has a comprehensive index of links to the Websites of literally hundreds of children's authors, sample lesson plans, and additional teacher resources. Author studies can be shared orally or in writing, depending on the age and sophistication of the students.

Thematic studies involve research on some theme (Pappas, Kiefer, and Levstik 1998 offer detailed guidance on planning thematic studies). Thematic units organized around concepts (e.g., pollution, things that live in the water, things that we need to live) offer the possibility of interdisciplinary study. Ideally, thematic units provide authentic reasons for reading, writing, and talking.

Responding to Text Through Art or Performance

Writing isn't the only way to respond to reading as a means of extending comprehension. Below arc a couple of examples of activities that involve nonwritten responses to text.

Symbolic Representation Interview (SRI) (Wilhelm 1997)

Using this technique, "students create cutouts or find objects to dramatize what they have read and how they have read it" (Wilhelm 1997, 43). Students use the cutouts or objects in a dramatic reading, sometimes explaining how their cutouts or objects represent characters, settings, and so on.

Visual Art

Any sort of visual artistic response (drawing, painting, clay sculpture, diorama, etc.) to reading can extend students' reading comprehension. For example, students can be asked to quickly sketch a scene or character from something they've read (Siegel 1984). The sketches are then used as the basis for further discussion of the text as students explain their drawings to their teachers or other students.

Partner (or Buddy) Reading

Partner reading can be done by students of similar or different reading levels. If the reading buddies are at similar levels, they read from the same text, perhaps chorally or taking turns (Fountas and Pinnell 1996). When a struggling reader is paired with a more capable reader, the students may also read together or take turns, or the more capable reader may listen to the struggling reader and offer appropriate feedback.

To be effective, students require explicit direction as they learn to support each other's reading. Curt Dudley-Marling's third graders often read in pairs, and he conducted several minilessons on how to respond to reading miscues, asking his students to talk about the kind of responses they found most helpful.

Effectively implemented, buddy reading positively affects the reading of both struggling readers and their more capable reading partners (Griffin 2002; Topping 1987, 1989). Melissa, a struggling reader, and Shirin, a stronger reader who reads below grade level, read together every day in Curt Dudley-Marling's reading workshop and both showed exceptional growth as readers by the end of the year.

Gradually Releasing Teacher Responsibility

One year, after having been a teacher for several years, Pat Paugh found that she was spending a great deal of time providing "extra" help to four girls who were struggling in her first-grade classroom. Pat realized that these girls were getting the bulk of her individual attention, often to the detriment of her other students. One day Pat asked the girls to take their assigned work to a corner of the room and help each other. She then conducted a number of reading conferences with her less demanding students. After about twenty minutes, the four girls excitedly appeared at the reading table, eager to show Pat what they had accomplished. They proudly presented a choral reading of the text they had

A Classroom Teacher's Guide to Struggling Readers

been struggling with. Working on their own, they had helped each other with unknown words and then practiced their "performance" of the story. Pat realized that her daily individual sessions with these girls had made them overdependent on her input.

Pat may have been reinforcing the girls' identities as "struggling readers" by not tapping their potential to work collaboratively as a means of taking some responsibility for their own learning. She found that the girls were able to draw on their collective knowledge to help each other while building confidence in themselves as readers. They went beyond the assignment to create their choral reading performance. Rather than "getting done," which had been their previous motivation, they were interacting and engaging in their reading in a meaningful way.

This experience doesn't tell the whole story of what's needed when classrooms are organized to allow students to work independently in groups or on their own. Many teachers' greatest challenge is getting students to choose and stick with books during independent reading. Another challenge is ensuring that students who are working in student-run literature discussions are engaged in talk that is rich and focused on the texts they've read. After watching a video of a well-run literature circle, one teacher commented, "This must be a setup. This would never happen in my classroom. The students would be fighting with each other the minute I left them alone!"

Inviting students to participate in their learning carries with it a gradual release of teacher responsibility (Pearson and Gallagher 1983). Simply asking students to "work together" or "read silently" assumes that they are prepared to choose texts and activities and focus on their learning independently. Independent reading can waste valuable classroom time if students don't understand the explicit expectations. This understanding is part of the learning process and occurs gradually.

In gradually releasing responsibility, a teacher moves from assuming "all the responsibility for performing a task . . . to a situation in which the students assume all of the responsibility" (Duke and Pearson 2002, 211). This gradual release may occur over a day, a week, or a semester. In organizing her instruction, the teacher includes lessons in which she mediates and supports students as they use and evaluate books and literacy-related activities independently.

Students, including struggling students, are able to take charge of and engage in effective literature discussions if (Kong and Pearson 2003):

- Teachers believe that the rich experience and knowledge students bring to their learning are important, and emphasize a classroom community in which mutual respect for the knowledge of others is valued.
- Students have the time and the opportunity to share their responses to literature and are encouraged to create meaning collaboratively.
- Students are pushed to think critically and reflect on what they have read by responding to thoughtful questions.
- Teachers employ multiple modes of teaching: presenting explicit instruction, modeling, coaching, scaffolding, facilitating students' discussions, at times participating as a group member.
- Teachers monitor independent discussions throughout the year and challenge students to maintain high expectations.

Look back at the various student activities going on in Mr. Garcia's classroom in Chapter 1. Several students are leaning against pillows, reading silently; two students are working at a listening center in the reading corner; two boys are sitting on the floor while a third classmate reads poems to them; several students are sitting on the rug with a collection of "scary books," discussing them excitedly; other students are completing a word sort; and one student is reading and writing notes at the message center. These activities have clear instructional goals and expectations, but it is important to remember that they are not specified in Mr. Garcia's lesson plan. Also, Mr. Garcia has spent a significant amount of time early in the year preparing his students for these independent activities. Finally, Mr. Garcia monitors his students' independent reading with ongoing assessment, supplemented by the students' self-assessment.

Students Take Ownership

Choosing Their Own Books

Students need to be taught how to choose "just right" books—that is, books that are not too hard or continuously too easy (many teach-

A Classroom Teacher's Guide to Struggling Readers

ers call this the Goldilocks method!). For example, Ms. Smith noticed that one of her third-grade boys picked up the same Clifford the Big Red Dog picture book (Norman Bridwell's series for Scholastic) day after day. While she was pleased to see him reading, she knew he needed to expand his interests and try new genres and more challenging texts. Ms. Smith chose several short chapter books from the classroom library: a few humorous ones and a realistic story with an animal as the central character. During a reading conference, she offered these to the boy while discussing things he liked and disliked reading about. She emphasized that she thought he was ready to try more challenging texts. The student chose one of the books and kept track of his reading using a self-assessment slip filled out after each SSR period (Rhodes 1993).

Keeping independent reading expectations high, while at the same time encouraging students' natural interests and choices, is necessary if students are to grow as readers. Sometimes teachers worry that they will "turn off" their students by suggesting different topics or more difficult books; however, it's important to do so, especially for struggling students. An element of choice can still be retained, and students will be able to see how they are growing as readers.

Another common issue related to choosing books is that students feel they need to read "big" or "heavy" books that are too difficult for them. Struggling students particularly attach prestige to the size and difficulty of books and often choose books that frustrate them. To grow as readers, students need to read texts that they can understand independently (Allington 2000; Calkins 2000), and teachers have to give readers the tools and strategies they need to make good choices. One quick strategy is "five fingers down." Students read the first page of a chapter book (or the first several pages of a picture book) and whenever they find a word they don't recognize, they fold a finger down. If they fold five fingers down before finishing the page or brief section, the text is likely to be to frustrating. Another strategy is for students to write down the pros and cons of choosing a particular book and then request a conference with their teacher or a peer to help decide whether a book is "just right." It's important that students who are struggling with grade-level texts have authentic texts to read at their level and be offered alternative ways (films, videos, or other media) to access content that is too difficult for them to read independently.

Reading Their World

In many elementary classrooms, reading environmental print is a collaborative activity. In one school in which Pat taught, teachers wrote poems, song lyrics, and student-created texts (interactive stories, for example) on large charts and asked students to read and reread these texts with partners. Partner reading of environmental print was introduced and modeled in every class beginning in preschool and was an expected independent activity through grade 5.

A first-grade teacher provided a special "pointer" for partners to use as they did their "literacy walk" (Fountas and Pinnell 1996). She found that students read together and to each other, enjoying the texts while practicing reading skills.

One of the third-grade teachers in this school wrote original songs using science and social studies themes, deliberately including appropriate vocabulary. Practicing these song lyrics, which were written on charts, was an authentic use of text and prompted the students to take ownership of reading, singing, and practicing new vocabulary.

Choosing and Designing Their Own Activities

Academic choice is an approach to organizing classrooms in which students not only choose activities to use to practice what they've been learning but also help construct those activities (Charney 2002; Fisher 2001).

In one school, classroom teachers and the school literacy specialist challenged students to design activities for practicing word study. Students' suggestions included traditional word lists and word sorts. However, as the teachers and students refined these activities, students hit upon changing the word sort into a sentence sort. As students took more ownership of their learning, they were also invited to help assess what and how they were learning. These activities contributed to their metacognitive understanding of literacy, something especially important for struggling readers.

Developing Metacognitive Awareness

Metacognition, literally thinking about one's thinking, plays an important role in student learning (Pintrich 2002). Students' metacognitive awareness of their literacy includes knowing strategies for different literacy tasks, knowing which strategies are most effective for particular tasks, and knowing how they will implement these strategies (Keene and Zimmerman 1997; Wilhelm 2001a). Metacogitive awareness also includes readers' understanding of their motivation for reading and a conscious awareness of their strengths and weaknesses as readers.

Metacognitive awareness can help a reader size up the learning setting and carry out a particular task. Pintrich (2002) refers to this as situational or conditional knowledge: for example, understanding that a multiple-choice test requires recalling a specific fact rather than overall information influences how a student prepares for such a test.

This book includes a number of examples of opportunities for students to reflect on and articulate what they know about reading: student/teacher conferences, student/student partner activities, and written responses and self-assessments. To support students' metacognitive awareness and help them internalize their learning strategies, strengths, and weaknesses, teachers need to explicitly label and discuss students' thinking, encouraging them to connect their thinking to their everyday learning activities.

Culminating reading workshop activities ask students to critique and reflect on their learning. These activities include whole-class sharing or debriefing sessions; ongoing, whole-class evaluations of student learning; and whole-school literacy celebrations.

Debriefing Sessions

Maura had been observing three ESL students in her classroom. She was troubled by their lack of interest in the English language books in the classroom library. When one of them found a book in which the story was written in both English and Spanish (the student's primary language), Maura listened as the little girl excitedly explained how she used the Spanish version to help her understand the English words. Maura was able to get a better sense of her student's first language literacy and the strategies the girl was using to make sense of Spanish and English text. As they talked together Maura labeled these strategies in an attempt to bring them into the girl's conscious awareness.

When discussions like these take place with the whole class at the end of independent reading, other students have the benefit of learning from their classmates' and their own learning. The role of the teacher in drawing attention to and noting such metacognitive conversation is critical. In the above example, Maura could have kept a chart available in the classroom to list students' strategies for future reference. There's an additional example of an end-of-workshop debriefing in Chapter 1: at the end of his reading workshop, Mr. Garcia invites his students to discuss any problems they had while they were reading.

Ongoing Debriefing During a Unit of Study

Much literacy learning occurs around units of study, whether in content areas (math, science, social studies, history, geography) or of literature genres and authors or literary elements. A popular frame for creating metacognitive awareness of prior knowledge and new learning about these topics is the K-W-L chart (Ogle 1986), which is divided into three columns:

- "What do we already know?" (K),
- "What do we still want to learn?" (W), and
- "What have we learned?" (L)

Regularly revisiting the chart as students complete various activities within the unit allows students to evaluate, reevaluate, and raise questions about their understanding and application of the knowledge in the unit.

As a first-grade teacher, Pat taught a half-year "central subject" study of the Middle Ages. She and her students kept track of their learning and their developing understanding using a set of questions she learned from Eleanor Duckworth (1987). As in K-W-L, Pat continually asked her students *What do you know? What surprises you? What questions do you have?* when her students encountered new ideas within this unit. She also encouraged her students to put their questions on sticky notes and keep them on a bulletin board. Often, weeks after asking a particular question, the student or a classmate would notice a reference to that question in a book or an activity, and the students would remove the question from the board and have a (usually animated!) discussion. This practice also encouraged "critical" questions like those of gender fairness (many of the girls wanted to know, "Does the prince always have to save the princess?") or Eurocentrisim (an African American student asked, "What was going on in Africa during this time?" and spurred a class visit to a local museum to view an exhibit of African and Asian armor).

Whole-School Celebrations

Celebrations are a means by which students can present their work from a unit of study more broadly to fellow students, parents, or community members. There is a wide range of these types of presentations, from monthly authors' teas at which students share their writing to annual fairs at which students present their individual or group research projects in various content areas. In responding to questions about their writing or their projects, students reflect on their learning process and explain their learning. An example of a celebration of reading might be a Multicultural Book Celebration: students and families choose books in which they "see themselves" (Nieto 1993) or that are important to their lives and share them with others in the school community. In any "celebration," it is the talk around learning and the labeling of that learning that add to students' repertoire of understanding about reading and literature.

If You Have to Use a Basal

Teachers and schools are challenged to provide the best instruction that will promote high levels of literacy in their students, but often the "answer" to this challenge remains elusive. Research on "best practice" and the folk wisdom found in schools often reinforce the myth that a given program will provide everything students need to learn to read, write, and think (Bartolome 1996). However, the achievement of students depends on their teachers, not a program (Darling-Hammond 1997). Only a knowledgeable use of materials that attends to the realities of the students as learners and the cultural context of the students' lives will lead to high achievement for all learners (Ladson-Billings 1995). While a basal or other commercial program can provide good resources for reading instruction, it is the informed decisions of a knowledgeable teacher as he or she uses these materials that will ultimately make a difference for students.

Nevertheless, if you are a teacher in a public elementary school, it's likely your school has adopted a basal reading program. Many teachers find themselves asking, *How closely should I follow the teacher's manual?* and, *What do I do with students whose needs are not being met by the basal curriculum?* The good news is, basal reading programs can be used to support struggling readers.

What's a Basal?

Basal readers are "sequential, all-inclusive set(s) of instructional materials that are intended to teach all children to read [and are organized around] a hierarchy of skills and a tightly controlled vocabulary" (Goodman et al. 1988, 1). Typically, basal reading programs include a weekly sequence of lessons for day 1 through day 5. The most popular basal programs include anthologies of stories and nonfiction selections, although it is common for the weekly lessons to focus on a single reading. Basal programs also tend to include a steady diet of workbooks and worksheets for students to "practice" skills they have been taught during the weekly lessons. Accompanying teacher manuals usually contain an assortment of lesson plans and assessments, sometimes with detailed scripts specifying precisely what teachers should say and when (naturally, teachers differ greatly in how closely they follow these scripts).

Basals are a reality teachers cannot ignore. If a basal reading program is part of the curriculum, they must decide how to use it: will they follow the suggested sequence of instruction or supplement it with trade books and additional instructional methods and assessments that focus on the unique learning needs of their students? For example, when a speech pathologist we know recommended that a second-grade teacher use the strategy of "repeated readings" with a struggling reader, the teacher rejected the advice, citing the scheduling demands of the basal reading program: "If Aaron reads the basal stories more than once, he'll get behind."

Scripted, one-size-fits-all programs will never be congenial to the wide range of instructional needs present in any classroom. The basal assumes that "learning to read" is a process in which teachers simply transmit information within a specific time frame. This format grossly misrepresents how children learn to read and ignores the diversity of literacy understanding students bring to their learning. To meet the needs of struggling readers effectively, teachers must use basal reading materials with discretion.

Using Basals with Struggling Readers

Some teachers who use basal programs feel they must follow them religiously, making sure that students read each selection and complete the practice materials or activities according to the instructions in the teachers manual. But despite the highly controlled design of the basal lessons, teachers generally have more flexibility than they realize in how or whether to use these materials. Certainly, there are teachers who are expected by their administrators to follow the basal script closely. In extreme cases, principals or reading coaches monitor teachers to see that they are on the right page on the right day.

But this is the exception. Few teachers slavishly follow a basal script. Nationally, no more than a quarter of the nation's elementary teachers claim to follow the basal closely (Education Market Research 2002). Many teachers, however, "find it useful to have basal materials and instructional suggestions to draw from, adapt, or extend as they craft lessons" (Bauman and Heubach 1996, 511). For example, an urban superintendent recently confided that his intent with regard to basal readers was for teachers to keep their sights on the district's reading plan and use them as *one set of resources* for achieving district reading goals.

Another teacher we met recently used basal materials as a source of topics and activities in connection with a unit on mapping for her third graders. She presented the topic, assessed her students' prior knowledge about mapping, asked them to construct their own learning activity relative to the topic, and then encouraged them to develop their own questions. She then compared the basal manual's lessons and questions with her students' ideas and suggestions. She found that her students became very involved in the lesson and took it very seriously and that the questions and activities they developed were more challenging and complex than those in the basal. By including her students' contributions and participation as a resource for learning, she encouraged them to think more deeply.

Teachers need to use basal materials selectively, judiciously, and critically to meet the needs of struggling students. Learning to read should always take place within a meaningful context, with the reader making sense of printed text in an active and purposeful way. Students' needs, not the basal curriculum, should drive reading instruction.

Teachers must choose materials that fit the needs of their students, not to try to fit students to a particular program.

Using the Basal with Discretion

Pat Paugh worked in "basal schools" during her fifteen years as a first-grade teacher. She found that treating reading as a sequential set of skills to be acquired prevented her from developing the understanding that she needed to look closely at her students as complex learners. Pat was aware that certain students' skills were below grade level, but in trying to fit the students to the basal she failed to evaluate students as readers in their own right. Later in her career, she learned to pay attention to students' language, background knowledge, understanding of and attitude toward reading, and sense of how to read for different purposes while closely monitoring the strategies they were using or not using to make sense of text. Pat's initial definition of "reading," which referenced sets of "basal skills," failed to provide her with enough specific information for teaching any of her students, especially struggling students.

Pat eventually learned how to overcome the limitations and use basals to accomplish her broader goals of encouraging active student involvement, building on students' existing background knowledge and experience, and conducting routine classroom assessments. She found that this orientation changed the nature of her reading instruction from reading as a subject area to literacy as a goal across the disciplines. Her new understanding also led her to develop curriculum in conjunction with her students, helping them take a more active role in their own learning.

Preserving an Active Role for Students

School literacy becomes meaningful to children when they take part in a conversation about what and how they learn. Children who are invited to contribute their background knowledge, experiences, and book choices to the literacy curriculum are more likely to become deeply engaged in texts (Dudley-Marling and Searle 1995). Teachers often complain about students whose only motivation is to "get through" their assigned reading rather than enter the world of the story or ask questions of informational texts that will extend their learning. If sequenced reading materials are the sole texts in a classroom, students come to view the goal of reading as something you do for the teacher and on which you are evaluated rather than as a means to understand, interpret, and act on the world (Education Department of Western Australia 1994).

Choosing books is an important way students can take ownership of and responsibility for their learning. Teachers who make a wide range of trade books available in the classroom and present minilessons on choosing good books for various purposes encourage student autonomy and, ultimately, engagement with regard to reading—a fundamental aspect of being literate (Cambourne 2002). Since it's expensive to purchase trade books for classroom libraries, basal anthologies that include a range of authentic literature can be a relatively economical way to augment the classroom library. Basal anthologies can also become part of text sets for literature circles. Teachers can draw on both trade books and basal anthologies to put together fiction, nonfiction, and poetry around a particular theme in conjunction with a literature, science, or social studies unit.

Building on Students' Background Knowledge and Experience

Valerie teaches in a high-achieving elementary school in a low-achieving, economically depressed school district whose student population encompasses children with a great many cultural and linguistic differences. She uses the basal reading program purchased by her school district, but she feels that neither the lessons nor the selections in the anthology of readings adequately relate to her students' background knowledge and experience. Valerie's teaching draws on years of professional experience, her ongoing assessment of her students, and her understanding of her students' cultural backgrounds and the community in which they and she live. As she conducts lessons she hopes will challenge her students to higher levels of reading achievement, Valerie supplements the basal materials and reading selections with a great many trade books that reflect the diversity in her classroom. At times she replaces text selections from the basal unit with trade books she feels better fit her goals and students' needs.

Valerie conceives of her literacy instruction as a conversation in which her students make real-life connections to the texts they read and in doing so realize that "their lives matter." For example, in Valerie's experience, the basal manual's activities for developing students' knowledge and vocabulary aren't always considerate of her students' background and experience. So although Valerie uses ideas from the basal manual to teach vocabulary and other reading skills, she also uses her morning meeting to encourage students to connect the text from the basal anthology they've been reading to their own experience, to other texts they've read, and to their general knowledge of the world (Keene and Zimmerman 1997). She provides a supportive scaffold that helps her students begin to shape their thinking about evaluating and connecting their present understanding as they build new understanding.

Valerie also makes sure that she links students' reading and writing activities to school-based literacy events such as monthly authors' circles. She uses supplemental materials provided in the basal program in accordance with her ongoing assessment of her students' needs. She finds these "extra" books and writing activities very helpful; however, she only occasionally uses the workbook pages and copies those pages instead of purchasing an entire workbook for each student.

Linking the Basal to Ongoing Classroom Assessment

The assessment/instruction cycle is the key to building students' competence and challenging them to go further. When using a basal reading program for instruction, it is still important to match instructional materials from the basal to students' needs rather than allow the scope and sequence of the basal lesson to determine student competence.

A first-grade teacher in one of Pat's university classes worries about how the school principal will evaluate her use of a newly adopted basal program. Although the principal expects her to start *all* her students at "day one," she always administers running records and other informal assessments to determine the instructional reading level of the individual students in her class. These assessments usually indicate that only *some* of her students have the level of skills assumed by the basal reading lessons. She often finds that a given basal story frustrates some of her students in their attempt to read it. She worries that as these students struggle to decode words, they will never develop strategies for making sense of whole texts. Also, inevitably, a few students can read the story independently; for them, the selection may not be sufficiently challenging, but they may still benefit from some of the related basal lessons on vocabulary and/or grammar.

In the end, this teacher finds that organizing her instruction around minilessons and guided reading informed by her own assessment and using the basal as one of many resources allows her to create a much more focused and flexible curriculum than the rigid and permanent "groupings" suggested by the basal would allow.

Understanding Children's Growth as Readers

Taking control of the basal rather than letting the basal determine how teachers label and teach their students has many benefits. These include a deep understanding of students' growth as readers. Rather than ranking reading ability as "on level" or "below level," teachers are able to talk to students, parents, and principals using specific information about students' progress. Rather than labeling a student as "struggling," teachers are able to report on what specific knowledge these students use in the process of reading and where they need to be challenged.

For example, just last week the first-grade teacher mentioned above used a story from the basal anthology but had her students develop their own questions and reread for information to meet instructional needs that she had identified from her assessments but that were not part of the basal lesson. When she takes the time to focus on meaning in this way, her students understand that their reading is purposeful and not just a matter of completing the lesson or getting through the day's assignment. This teacher uses her routine assessments to ensure that her students are active participants in their learning and that what she's teaching, whether from the basal or not, responds to her students' particular instructional needs.

When Teachers Don't Have Much Flexibility

Some teachers are required to follow a scripted reading program closely. Some are even told how many minutes per day they need to devote to

A Classroom Teacher's Guide to Struggling Readers

basal instruction. These kinds of constraints make it difficult, perhaps even impossible, to implement the kind of workshop approach for reading instruction we're discussing in this book. One-size-fits-all programs will never be considerate of the diverse needs of struggling readers, however, and teachers have a responsibility, at a minimum, to augment these programs in order to provide the "frequent, intensive, explicit, and individualized support and direction" struggling readers require. This is a significant challenge.

Freeing a Block of Time for Reading Workshop

By satisfying the requirements of the basal reading program as efficiently as possible, teachers may be able to free a block of time for a reading workshop. Even thirty minutes a day of independent reading is better than no independent reading at all. If it isn't possible to schedule independent reading each day, then how about two or three days a week? Pat scheduled one session a week in her first-grade classroom for group discussions of a trade book chosen from her classroom collection. She also replaced some of the basal seatwork with teacher- and student-designed independent work related to these books.

Developing an Integrated, Interdisciplinary Framework for Language Arts Using the Reading Workshop Model

Organizing literature study or the social studies and science curriculums around thematic inquiry gives students frequent opportunities to read and write for extended periods as they explore various topics individually or in small groups (Hoyt 2002 and Pappas, Kiefer, and Levstik 1998 are excellent resources for organizing content-based language arts classrooms). The strategies we've discussed as part of a reading workshop can just as easily be implemented within an integrated language arts framework. Ideas include:

- Read-alouds with informational texts.
- Minilessons and reading conferences that model and support explicit reading strategies using informational/nonfiction books.
- Guided reading, shared reading, and literature circles using informational/nonfiction texts.

These formats work as well with informational texts as with fiction (conversely, reading workshop should of course include informational texts). Linda Hoyt (2002) discusses using shared reading of informational texts to teach everything from letter recognition, letter/sound correspondence, and phonemic awareness to rereading to check for meaning, text previewing, and critical reading strategies. In an integrated framework, teachers can support both learning to read and reading to learn. As a means of extending struggling students' opportunities to read and write—with the support of their teachers—an integrated approach to language arts is a powerful way to organize any classroom, even those that include daily reading workshops.

Using Practice Sheets or Seatwork to Support Authentic Tasks

Using the practice sheets or seatwork provided by a basal program in more authentic ways is another means by which to direct the program toward students' needs. When applicable, basal worksheets may be used to introduce a task. For example, basal-program practice activities may include letter writing, looking at punctuation when editing student work, or mapping information for a report. After being introduced to these structures through the basal worksheets, students can use these skills in literacy activities directly connected to their meaningful use of printed texts.

Guidelines for Selecting Basal Reading Programs

Not long ago, a Boston-area school district invited us to help them select a new basal reading program for all the schools in the district. Putting aside our prejudices about basals, we urged the teachers on the adoption committee to pay attention to how they would use the basal program to meet the learning needs of all their students. We also urged them to pay attention to the program's benefits and obstacles for their struggling students. Toward this end, we created the following framework for evaluating commercial reading programs.

Definition of Reading

1. What definition of reading is implicit in the program? Is reading conceived as a collection of discrete skills or something more complex? What evidence of this definition can you find in the teacher and student materials?
2. How does the definition of reading underpinning the program compare with the definition of reading implicit in district/state frameworks? Clearly, it is a disadvantage to adopt reading programs whose definition of reading is at odds with district or state language arts frameworks, but this does happen. What specific connections can you find? What connections are not there or conflict?

The Roles of Teachers and Students

1. What is the role of the teacher? Are teachers merely *managers* of the materials, or are they able to exercise some degree of professional discretion that draws on their knowledge and experience? How much of the program depends on the teachers' using a script? How much of the program allows for teachers' flexible use of the materials? In general, reading programs that position teachers as technicians should be resisted.
2. What is the role of the student? Are the students passive, or do they have a role in selecting, interpreting, and evaluating reading materials? A significant body of theory and research indicates that deep learning is related to active, sustained engagement; a more passive student role is associated with superficial, ephemeral learning (Cambourne 1988, 2002). Does the curriculum ask students to engage with and act on texts in meaningful ways, such as develop their own questions, offer opinions, engage with multiple perspectives, or even consider what texts might be missing?

Assessment

1. How is reading assessed? By whom? Does the program provide for ongoing assessment of students? Do the assessment tools fit easily into teachers' and students' daily routines?
2. How is assessment linked to instruction? Good assessment must inform day-to-day instruction. Normative assessments that

merely compare students are never much help in planning instruction.

3. What definition of reading is implicit in assessment materials (and does it match the definition of reading underpinning the instructional materials)? A program that limits assessment to the mastery of discrete skills assumes that reading equals the mastery of skills.

4. How does the program relate to district/state/national (NCTE/IRA) language arts frameworks or standards? All teachers are accountable to local and state standards, and most basal publishers go to extraordinary (and often quite creative) lengths to link their materials to these standards. Local adoption committees need to examine the credibility of these claims. (For example, one publisher asserts that asking a series of simple questions after students have read a six-line passage along the lines of "Nan can go with mom/Fan cannot" supports the development of reading comprehension and critical thinking—a rather dubious claim.) Do the actual tasks presented reasonably fit the stated goals?

Research Support

1. What is the research base of the program? This is a difficult question for most teachers to consider. Increasingly, teachers have a good background in research that enables them to evaluate educational research critically, but few have the time. But at least some effort ought to be made to evaluate the research claims by publishers. For example, all publishers now include "decodable" books in their materials and claim that this is based on research—even though there appears to be no research supporting the efficacy of decodable texts in beginning reading instruction (Allington and Woodside-Jiron 1998). Also, since publishing is a business, research functions as a marketing device. No publisher is going to share negative evidence, even if it exists.

2. Is there independent research in support of the program or has research been conducted largely by the publisher or the authors of the program? Again, publishers undertake research from a marketing perspective, so research that has been supported by the publishers should be evaluated carefully.

A Classroom Teacher's Guide to Struggling Readers

3. How is reading defined in this research? This is perhaps the key issue in controversies over the meaning of reading research. How reading is measured (and, by implication, defined) in reading research makes all the difference in what we make of it. If a study supporting a particular reading strategy (or reading program) measures reading progress in terms of sounding out nonsense words, for example, we might not get too excited by its claims of success if we believe that reading involves much more than mastering phonics.

4. For whom is the program effective? Who was included in the research sample(s)? If the students in the research sample don't look like our students, we may justly wonder and worry about the impact the program would have on our class.

Meeting the Needs of Diverse Learners

1. What accommodations are made for struggling readers? Too often commercial reading programs accommodate struggling readers only through supplemental worksheets and alternative readings without modifying instructional goals or the pace of instruction. Five-day lesson cycles in which everyone is supposed to be in the same place by the end of the week do not consider the diverse needs of struggling readers. Are students who struggle segregated in permanent groups or given materials that offer less rich experiences or content?

2. What accommodations are made for exceptionally strong readers? It is as ridiculous a waste of time to teach children what they already know as it is to teach skills students aren't ready to learn. An effective reading program must accommodate the needs of all students, including the most able.

3. How well do the materials accommodate students' linguistic and cultural differences? Are English language learners able to access rich content and the language needed for academic literacy as they learn English, or are they forced to wait until they are proficient in English before they are able to engage fully in the subject matter? Also, are the claims made relative to a diversified curriculum meaningful for the students you teach? In some cases, special lessons are provided for English language learners, but those lessons do not accommodate *every* English language

learner. Again, it is important that the (expensive) resources provided in any commercial reading program support the diverse needs of all students, not just some mythical average student.

Revaluing Struggling Readers

When children fail to learn to read as soon as they are expected to (which is much earlier than it used to be) or as well as they are expected to, the first question many school officials—and parents and caregivers as well—tend to ask is, what's wrong with her (or him)? Presumably, learning problems reside *in the heads of struggling learners* and determining "what's wrong" will lead to instruction designed to fix, or at least overcome, students' learning deficiencies.

Everyone loses when we pathologize learning difficulties in this way. There is no convincing evidence that "diagnosing" learning problems leads directly (or even indirectly) to effective instructional strategies. Struggling readers do require frequent, intensive, explicit, and individualized support and direction, but there is no evidence that they require instruction that is qualitatively different from their peers. No one has found a set of strategies for teaching reading that are specific to the needs of struggling readers. In fact, since *different reading instruction leads to students learning different things,* differentiated instruction can create—or at least aggravate—reading problems by denying some students access to crucial reading experiences.

All readers need to learn phonics skills, for example, but overemphasizing these skills can limit opportunities for some struggling readers to read connected text, a critical experience in learning to read (Allington 2000). Similarly, poor readers are more likely to be presented lessons that emphasize words, sounds, and letters—often out of context—while good readers, even at the same developmental level, are more likely to experience lessons that emphasize meaning (Allington 1980). According to Frank Smith (1998), the deprivation of meaningful experience makes learning more difficult for struggling learners by obscuring the fundamental insight for beginning readers: reading makes sense.

In general, differentiated instruction creates a self-fulfilling prophecy:

- A student doesn't learn to read as quickly or as easily as expected.
- The student is assigned to a low or remedial reading group or special education class.
- Instruction focuses on a scope and sequence of "basic" skills to the exclusion of other critical learning opportunities (e.g., reading books and other connected text).
- The student gets better at the "basic" skills but falls further and further behind in other areas of reading (e.g., comprehension).

Or, as Hiebert (1983) puts it, once a bluejay, always a bluejay.

Revaluing learners isn't simply a matter of believing in children or not believing in them. Children aren't going to be more or less competent readers merely because teachers wish it. What this stance does, however, is challenge teachers to consider broadly the range of factors that can influence children's performance in school and endeavor to affect those factors over which they have the most control. Teachers have the least control over the dispositions, ability, and experiences students bring with them to school. They can, however, affect the instructional task and how they initiate and respond to students' actions.

Alternative Models of Struggling Readers

Situating learning difficulties *in the heads* of students contributes to the creation of contexts that deny struggling readers opportunities to see themselves—and be seen by others—as competent learners. From this point of view, learning problems emerge in the complex interaction of teachers and students in the context of lessons and materials in a place called school. As a sociologist might put it, interacting with particular people in particular places in particular ways makes us into particular kinds of people, including competent or incompetent learners (Gergen 1990). This complicated perspective contradicts the commonsense notion that each of us has an identity independent of social context.

To make it clearer how instructional contexts contribute to our sense of learners as competent or not competent, let's look at two examples of a student and a teacher working with very different kinds of reading lessons with dramatically different effects on learner identity.

Example 1

Regis is a third grader in a self-contained class for students with learning disabilities. Mrs. Stroh, his teacher, is talking with him about a reading worksheet he began the previous day.

Mrs. Stroh: Show me all of the pictures that begin with /m/. [*She points to a picture of a car.*] Does this begin with /m/, Regis?

Regis: Nope.

Mrs. Stroh: I want you to go through the page. Show me the pictures that begin with /m/. [*Regis points to the pictures on the page that begin with /m/.*] All right. You missed one. See if you can find the one you missed.

Regis: [*Looks the page over for roughly one minute.*] No. Yeah.

Mrs. Stroh: Where is it? Where is the one you missed?

Regis: Right here. [*He points to a picture of a monkey.*]

Mrs. Stroh: No, you showed me that one before. What's this? [*She points to a picture of a match.*]

Regis: I don't know. What it is?

Mrs. Stroh: We talked about that yesterday, Regis. What is it that you use to start a fire? [*Pause.*] Do you have a fireplace? When you want to build a fire in the fireplace what do you have to have?

Regis: This thing. [*He points to the picture of the match.*]

Mrs. Stroh: Yes, I know you have to have that thing, but what's it called? Who starts the fires in your house?

Regis:	My grandpa gets the fire to—
Mrs. Stroh:	[*Interrupting*] Does he ever say, bring me a ____?
Regis:	Wood.
Mrs. Stroh:	Well, probably, yes. Does he ever say, bring me a match, please?
Regis:	No, he doesn't say that.
Mrs. Stroh:	Oh, he doesn't say *that*. What is *that*?
Regis:	He sometimes, when he goes down in the basement, sometimes I help him carry up the wood, get the wood, and bring it upstairs to the fire.
Mrs. Stroh:	Good. Get that ____.
Regis:	Wood.
Mrs. Stroh:	What did I just say?
Regis:	I don't know. . . . I couldn't hear you.
Mrs. Stroh:	Oh yes. You could hear me. What did I say? Does Grandpa ever ask you to bring him a ____?
Regis:	Wood.
Mrs. Stroh:	Match. [*She is clearly exasperated.*]
Regis:	A match.
Mrs. Stroh:	Uh-huh. That word, *match*, has different meanings. [*Mrs. Stroh goes on to talk with Regis about the different meanings of* match.]

Mrs. Stroh is struggling to get Regis to recall the word *match*. It isn't clear whether Regis has forgotten the word or if he merely doesn't recognize the drawing of the match on the worksheet. Or perhaps Regis isn't sure what Mrs. Stroh wants from him. Certainly if someone in authority showed us a picture of a match and asked us to identify it, we might be a bit uncertain about what was expected (is this a trick? it's clearly a picture of a match so maybe there is more to this than is immediately apparent). We might respond cautiously, just as Regis does. It could also be that Regis is just being uncooperative or resistant. But Mrs. Stroh concludes that Regis cannot recall the word *match*. This leads her to invoke a guess-what-I'm-thinking script using the familiar initiation–response–evaluation pattern (teacher asks a question, student responds, teacher evaluates student's response—Barnes 1976), which anyone who has gone to school will recognize.

Whatever Regis's motivation, there are a couple of ways to interpret this interaction. From an in-the-head deficit perspective, the problem belongs to Regis, whose "learning disability" has manifested itself as a difficulty with "word finding." This is clearly how Mrs. Stroh sees it. Alternatively, from the social constructivist perspective that guides our work with struggling readers, the task (the worksheet), the setting (a classroom), and the interaction between Mrs. Stroh and Regis are all instrumental in producing (or reproducing) Mrs. Stroh's identity as "teacher" and Regis's identity as a "struggling reader." These perceived identities, in turn, influence the moves that Regis and Mrs. Stroh make during their interaction. Regis's moves are affected by his sense of the task and of Mrs. Stroh as a teacher (and a particular kind of teacher at that). The significance Mrs. Stroh attaches to Regis's response ("I don't know. What is it?") to her question "What's this?" is almost certainly affected by his identity as a "struggling learner" (a conclusion supported during a subsequent interview with Mrs. Stroh). If a different label were attached to Regis—"gifted," for example—Mrs. Stroh would likely attach a very different meaning to his "I don't know." She might respond with something like, "I know it's hard to tell from the picture, but it's a match." She almost certainly would not have assumed that "I don't know" signified a word-finding problem.

The initiation–response–evaluation framework Mrs. Stroh uses to address Regis's "word-finding" problem also plays a role in structuring their interaction. In this context, whatever Regis might say, all that matters is the "correct" answer (*match*). The shape and meaning of this interaction also depends on its being performed in a school. It is unlikely Regis's behavior would have the same meaning in other contexts. In any case, the guess-what-I'm-thinking paradigm would seem odd in any other setting. As it turns out, this is just the right task, performed at the right time and in the right place, to make Regis's learning problem visible. Certainly, Regis plays an important role in this struggling-reader performance, but it is a performance he could not have accomplished on his own. The task, the setting, and the interaction between Mrs. Stroh and Regis are perfectly orchestrated to reveal a learning problem. Arguably, a shift in the task or the interactions between the participants could have disrupted this well-choreographed event, producing a different learning identity for Regis.

Example 2

The following transcript is excerpted from a weeklong discussion (one and half hours a day) of a short story read by a fourth-grade class in an urban school district. Many of the students in this class had been identified as ESL learners and/or having special needs. The story is a challenging text that was first read to the class by their teacher, Mr. Jones, after which the students read the story twice on their own. Mr. Jones then worked to clarify the meaning of confusing words or phrases. Mr. Jones has been trained in the Junior Great Books program, which is "proven to help students develop the essential skills of reading carefully, thinking critically, listening intently, and speaking and writing persuasively" (Great Books Foundation 2004). In this excerpt, Mr. Jones and his students discuss an ambiguous event in the story: whether or not the character named Scho fell from a tree on his own or if he was pushed by one of the other characters in the story.

Mr. Jones: Jean, you're smiling. What do you think?

Jean: Well, I'm thinkin' that he fell—he didn't fall on purpose.

Mr. Jones: Why, why not Jean?

Jean: Because . . . on page six where Monk said that he's sorry . . . that he's sorry for making him fall.

Mr. Jones: You know what I'm curious about? What he means by the word *made*. "I didn't mean to make you fall." What does that mean?

Jeremy: Well, the "mean" there, the "mean" there means that he didn't want it to happen, I think.

Mr. Jones: Jean, will you read that place again?

Jean: Sure. "'I'm sorry Scho,' Monk said. 'I didn't mean to make, to make you fall.'"

Mr. Jones: "I didn't mean to make you fall."

Lynette: I think he *did* mean to make him fall.

Jacob: Wait a minute. Maybe when Monk was coming up the branch, he could have grabbed onto the branch that Scho was sitting on top of and he, Scho, could have let go of the one he was hanging onto and he could of fell.

A Classroom Teacher's Guide to Struggling Readers

Mr. Jones: That still doesn't really help us out with that. Why does he say, "I didn't mean to make you fall"?

Niyasha: He probably means that when he say, when he was threatening him to be quiet and quiet and quiet up inside the tree, Scho thought he was gonna come and push him so he might have let go because he was scared that Monk was *gonna* push him.

Mr. Jones: So how does that—if Scho lets go—this is really interesting. I mean this is why it's such a puzzle to me. If Scho lets go because he thinks Monk is going to push him, why does Monk say, "I'm sorry, I didn't mean to make you fall"?

Malaysha: Maybe, maybe because when he found, he was going down to say I'm sorry . . . since he saw Scho had maybe got hurt and he wanted to say, "I'm sorry, I didn't mean to push you," so he could say—instead of—Scho knows he didn't push him but he just said the I'm sorry so Scho'll think that he did push him, wh—when he gets up.

Mr. Jones: Why would he want that to happen?

Malaysha: Because if he thinks that he pushed him and if Monk pushed him, he'll know what happened, instead of just saying that he fell by hisself—self and before Monk and "the crazy kid" had just fell by hisself, so he probably didn't push him but he was just saying— apologize so he would think that he did.

Lynette: I agree with Malaysha that, um, that, um, Monk really didn't make him fall, but, in a way I disagree, because, um. . . .

Mr. Jones: Oh, can you repeat that? Can you repeat that for me? For all of us, I mean.

Lynette: I disagree and I agree with Malaysha because—

Mr. Jones: I disagree *and* agree. Okay.

Lynette: —with Malaysha because um, and, um, in, in the part of the story, I think it was on page six, they um, um, Monk was shaking the branches, branches because . . . Scho wouldn't leave them alone or something like that. And, um, and when, um, Scho fell down from the tree and he hurt himself, um, when Monk was shaking the branches I think that Scho thought . . . that Monk pushed him and that's why, um, Monk said, "I'm sorry, Scho, I didn't mean to make you fall."

Jeremy: I have something for what Niyasha said. Niyasha, remember what you said when, um, that . . . you thought that Scho had fallen out because Scho thought that Monk was gonna push him?

Niyasha: Yeah.

Jeremy: Why would Scho push, uh, jump . . . or let go . . . when he know that he could get hurt?

Niyasha: He might have let go because he was scared that Monk was gonna push him. So he let go, so he could jump by himself without Monk pushing him because, well, if Monk pushed him he might have got hurt even *more*.

Jean: I agree with Niyasha that, well, I think that maybe he was trying to get out 'cuz Monk said that he was going to move the branch and he was trying to get out. Maybe he slipped and, um, and fell.

Jacob: If you're sitting up in a tree, Jean, how can you slip and fall?

Enrique: Maybe, if Monk, if Monk was holding onto the same branch and . . . and Scho thought he was going to shake the branch, but he jumped off before he could, so that if Monk could've pushed him off the branch and then Scho wouldn't have been able to hold his balance, but when he jumped off he might've, he might've been able to keep his balance.

Mr. Jones: So did he fall on purpose or not?

This brief excerpt doesn't capture the rich participation of these fourth graders and the increasing sophistication of their engagement over the course of the week as they learned to use the text to develop and support their arguments. It does, however, offer a distinctly different vision of students, particularly struggling readers and writers. An engaging, challenging text and a particular set of moves by Mr. Jones

A Classroom Teacher's Guide to Struggling Readers

helps construct an identity for these students that emphasizes their intelligence, verbal skill, curiosity, and learning potential. Mr. Jones departs from the initiation–response–evaluation framework by abandoning the evaluation role in favor of "interested listener." Rather than positioning himself as someone on the lookout for deficits in need of remediation, Mr. Jones establishes himself as being genuinely curious about what his students have to say. He deliberately avoids any form of evaluation, using questions both to elicit student responses and to scaffold the development of the intellectual tools students needed for deep engagement with the text (for example, he routinely asks students to refer to the text to support their arguments). Mr. Jones also uses "wait time" effectively, often as a means of getting students to talk to one another and not just to him. The task, the students, and a deliberate set of conversational moves by Mr. Jones interact to construct this group of students as "smart" (Miller 1993).

Dancing to a New Tune

Instructional interactions between teachers and students are like a series of dance steps. In the case of Regis and Mrs. Stroh, Mrs. Stroh makes the first move by asking, "What's this?" as she points to a picture of a match. Regis responds, "I don't know. What is it?" Over the course of their interaction, Regis and Mrs. Stroh's "dance" positions Regis as exhibiting a learning problem. Just as the physical setting for a dance (a crowded dance floor, for example, or streamers hanging from the ceiling) and the props the dancers use (top hats and canes, for example) determine its shape and meaning, the task at the heart of Regis's and Mrs. Stroh's interaction—a worksheet—also affects Regis's performance. Overall, the task, the setting, and the participants work together to give shape and meaning to Regis's and Mrs. Stroh's actions— Regis has a learning problem.

Certainly, Regis plays a role in the construction of this dance, but it is Mrs. Stroh who "leads," who has the power in their relationship. If she had led differently, had introduced a different set of moves, the dance—and the dancers—would likely have looked very different. Different instructional materials—props—would also have had an effect on their interaction and perhaps on how Mrs. Stroh interpreted Regis's behavior.

Arguably, the principal difference between the instructional dance performed by Regis and Mrs. Stroh and the one performed by Mr. Jones and his students is the nature of the instructional material (an engaging story versus a worksheet emphasizing initial sounds) and how the teachers choose to lead the conversation. Mrs. Stroh initiates a series of moves she hopes will lead Regis toward the "correct" answer, to guess what she is thinking. For Mr. Jones, there is no right answer. His moves are calculated to engage his students in thoughtful conversation about the story they have read—specifically, whether or not Scho has fallen "on purpose"—as a way to help his students develop higher levels of reading comprehension.

Just as a dancer can affect our perceptions of her or his partner, Mr. Jones and Mrs. Stroh significantly affect the learning identity we attribute to their students. Regis and his teacher perform a series of well-coordinated actions that reinforce his identity as "not competent." Mr. Jones and his students execute a set of coordinated moves that present students as thoughtful, engaged, and highly competent (even though, in other settings, these students may often have been perceived as "not competent").

What does this mean for teachers who want to offer high-quality instruction for struggling readers? To begin with, learning and learning problems do not merely reside in the heads of our students. Teacher actions and the instructional context also play a significant role in whether students are perceived as *competent* or *not competent*. Students cannot manifest their learning "problems" on their own. Understanding that the manifestation of a learning problem is a complex act involving teachers, students, tasks, and setting leads to asking different sorts of questions when learning breaks down (that is, when children do not appear smart). Instead of asking, *What's wrong with this student?* teachers might ask, *What's going on here? What factors are contributing to the student's performing poorly and which of those are under my control?*

If we assume that children are naturally bright, inquisitive, and interesting, we should suspect evidence to the contrary. The question isn't *whether* students like Regis are bright, curious, and interesting but, rather, *what makes them* smart, curious, and interesting—or, alternatively, what makes them appear to be dull and uninterested. It isn't *if*

Regis is smart but *when* he is smart—that is, what makes him smart (Miller 1993)? The aim isn't to fix learners who are somehow deficient but to build on children's intelligence and interests.

This what's-happening-here stance, arising from the belief that all children are smart, might have led to a very different sort of interaction between Regis and Mrs. Stroh. Perhaps Mrs. Stroh wouldn't have automatically assumed that Regis's "I don't know" in response to her "What is this?" indicated a word-finding problem. She would have at least considered the effect of the task and the moves she made on Regis's behavior. She may have drawn on his existing language skill as a foundation for challenging Regis to develop more complex language and richer vocabulary instead of treating his language as a deficit.

The what's-happening-here stance led Mr. Jones to identify moves that were most and least productive. He considered the role of the task and the quality of his own contributions to the discussion. He asked himself: *Could I have asked more productive questions? Did I give students enough time to formulate their thoughts? What could I do differently next time? What additional support can I offer to help students develop the intellectual tools to be able to engage deeply with texts and contribute to the discussion?*

Beginning with the assumption that all children are, indeed, smart, displays a respect for students, their experiences, their families, and the communities from which they come. Children know when we respect them—and they know when they are not being respected. Respect is fundamental to teaching all children, whatever their abilities or backgrounds. If we do not respect the students with whom we work, or are unable to show it, we will never be particularly successful teachers.

References

Allington, R. L. 2000. *What Really Matters for Struggling Readers: Designing Research-Based Programs.* New York: Longman.

———. 1980. "Teacher Interruption Behaviors During Primary-Grade Oral Reading." *Journal of Educational Psychology* 72: 371–77.

Allington, R. L., and P. Johnston. 2001. "What Do We Know About Effective Fourth-Grade Teachers and Their Classrooms?" In *Learning to Teach Reading: Setting the Research Agenda,* edited by C. Roller, 150–65. Newark, DE: International Reading Association.

Allington, R. L., and H. Woodside-Jiron. 1998. "Decodable Text in Beginning Reading: Are Mandates and Policy Based on Research?" *ERS Spectrum* 16 (2): 3–11.

Barnes, D. 1976. *From Communication to Curriculum.* New York: Penguin.

Barr, M., D. Craig, D. Fisette, and M. Syverson. 1999. *Assessing Literacy with the Learning Record: A Handbook for Teachers, Grades K–6.* Portsmouth, NH: Heinemann.

Bartolome, L. I. 1996. "Beyond the Methods Fetish: Toward a Humanizing Pedagogy." In *Breaking Free: The Transformative Power of Critical Pedagogy,* edited by P. Leistyna, A. Woodrum, and S. A. Sherblom. Cambridge, MA: Harvard Educational Review.

Baumann, J. F., and K. M. Heubach. 1996. "Do Basal Readers Deskill Teachers? A National Survey of Educators' Use and Opinions of Basals." *The Elementary School Journal* 96: 511–26.

Baumann, J. F., L. A. Jones, and N. Siefert-Kessell. 1993. "Using Think-Aloud to Enhance Children's Comprehension Monitoring Abilities." *The Reading Teacher* 47: 184–93.

Beaver, J. 2001. *Developmental Reading Assessment K–3*. Parsippany, NJ: Celebration/Pearson Learning.

Caldwell, J., and M. P. Ford. 2002. *Where Have All the Bluebirds Gone? How to Soar with Flexible Grouping*. Portsmouth, NH: Heinemann.

Calkins, L. 2000. *The Art of Teaching Reading*. New York: Longman.

Calkins, L., K. Montgomery, and D. Santman. 1998. *A Teacher's Guide to Standardized Reading Tests: Knowledge Is Power*. Portsmouth, NH: Heinemann.

Cambourne, B. 2002. "Conditions for Literacy Learning." *Reading Teacher* 55: 758–62.

———. 1988. *Whole Story: Natural Learning and the Aquisition of Literacy*. New York: Ashton Scholastic.

Cameron, A. 1989. *The Stories Julian Tells*. New York: Yearling.

Charney, R. S. 2002. *Teaching Children to Care: Classroom Management for Ethical and Academic Growth, K–8*. Rev. ed. Greenfield, MA: Northeast Foundation for Children.

Clarke, M. A., W. A. Davis, L. K. Rhodes, and E. Baker. 1995. *Creating Coherence: High Achieving Classrooms for Minority Students*. Preliminary report research conducted under U.S. Department of Education OERI Field Initiates Studies Program, Grant R117E30244. Denver, CO: University of Colorado–Denver.

Clay, M. M. 1993. *An Observation Survey of Early Literacy Achievement*. Portsmouth, NH: Heinemann.

Clements, A. 1999. *The Landry News*. Illustrated by S. Murdocca. New York: Simon & Schuster Books for Young Readers.

———. 1998. *Frindle*. Illustrated by Brian Selznick. New York: Aladdin Library.

Clymer, S. 1999. *There's a Tarantula in My Homework*. Illustrated by P. Casale. New York: Little Apple/Scholastic.

Coles, G. 2003. *Reading the Naked Truth: Literacy, Legislation, and Lies*. Portsmouth, NH: Heinemann.

Cooper, J. D., and N. D. Kiger. 2001. *Literacy Assessment: Helping Teachers Plan Instruction*. Boston: Houghton Mifflin.

Cronin, D. 2000. *Click, Clack, Moo: Cows That Type*. Illustrated by B. Lewin. New York: Simon and Schuster Children's.

Cunningham, P. M. 2000. *Phonics They Use: Words for Reading and Writing*. 3d ed. New York: Longman.

Dahl, R. 2000. *James and the Giant Peach*. New York: Penguin.

Darling-Hammond, L. 1997. *The Right to Learn: A Blueprint for Creating Schools That Work*. San Francisco: Jossey-Bass.

Dawson, M. M. 1987. "Beyond Ability Grouping: A Review of the Effectiveness of Ability Grouping and Its Alternatives." *School Psychology Review* 16: 348–69.

de Paola, T. 1975. *Strega Nona*. New York: Prentice Hall.

Duckworth, E. 1987. "*The Having of Wonderful Ideas and Other Essays on Teaching and Learning*." New York: Teachers College Press.

Dudley-Marling, C. 1997. *Living with Uncertainty: The Messy Reality of Classroom Practice*. Portsmouth, NH: Heinemann.

Dudley-Marling, C., and D. Searle. 1995. *Who Owns Learning? Questions of Autonomy, Choice, and Control*. Portsmouth, NH: Heinemann.

Duffy, G. G., and J. V. Hoffman. 1999. "In Pursuit of an Illusion: The Flawed Search for a Perfect Method." *The Reading Teacher* 53: 10–16.

Duke, N., and P. D. Pearson. 2002. "Effective Practices for Developing Reading Comprehension." In *What Research Has to Say About Reading Instruction*, 3d ed, edited by A. Farstrup and J. Samuels, 205–42. Newark, DE: International Reading Association.

Dykstra, R. 1968. "Summary of the Second-Grade Phase of the Cooperative Research Program in Primary Reading Instruction." *Reading Research Quarterly* 4: 49–70.

Edmondson, J., and P. Shannon. 2002. "The Will of the People." *The Reading Teacher* 55: 452–54.

Education Department of Western Australia. 1994. *First Steps Reading: Resource Book*. Portsmouth, NH: Heinemann.

Education Market Research. 2002. *The Complete K–12 Report: Market Facts and Segment Analyses, 2002*. New York: Education Market Research.

Fisher, R. 2001. "Choosing Choice: How a Third-Grade Teacher Learned to Integrate Academic Choice into a Prescribed Curriculum." *Responsive Classroom Newsletter* 13 (4).

Fountas, I. C., and G. S. Pinnell. 1996. *Guided Reading: Good First Teaching for All Children.* Portsmouth, NH: Heinemann.

Fox, M. 1989. *Wilfrid Gordon McDonald Partridge.* Brooklyn, NY: Kane/Miller.

Garan, E. 2002. *Resisting Reading Mandates: How to Triumph with the Truth.* Portsmouth, NH: Heinemann.

Gee, J. P. 1991. *Social Linguistics and Literacies: Ideology in Discourses.* Philadelphia: Taylor and Francis.

Gergen, K. J. 1990. "Social Understanding and the Inscription of Self." In *Cultural Psychology: Essays on Comparative Human Development*, edited by J. W. Stigler, R. A. Shweder, and G. Herdt, 569–606. New York: Cambridge University Press.

Goodman, K. S., P. Shannon, Y. Freeman, and S. Murphy. 1988. *Report Card on Basal Readers.* Katonah, NY: Richard C. Owen.

Goodman, Y. M. 1978. "Kidwatching: An Alternative to Testing." *National Elementary Principal* 57: 41–45.

Goodman, Y. M., D. J. Watson, and C. L. Burke. 1987. *Reading Miscue Inventory: Alternative Procedures.* Katonah, NY: Richard C. Owen.

Great Books Foundation. 2004. "Junior Great Books: Students Reading and Discussion Literature." Available online at *www.greatbooks.org/programs/junior/index.html.*

Griffin, M. L. 2002. "Why Don't You Use Your Finger? Paired Reading in First Grade." *The Reading Teacher* 55: 766–74.

Hansen, J. 1998. *When Learners Evaluate.* Portsmouth, NH: Heinemann.

Hiebert, E. H. 1983. "An Examination of Ability Grouping for Reading Instruction." *Reading Research Quarterly* 18: 231–55.

Hindley, J. 1998. *Inside Reading and Writing Workshops.* Video. York, ME: Stenhouse.

Hoffman, J. V., N. L. Roser, and J. Battle. 1993. "Reading Aloud in Classrooms: From the Modal Toward a 'Model.'" *The Reading Teacher* 46: 496–503.

Holdaway, D. 1982. "Shared Book Experience: Teaching Reading Using Favorite Books." *Theory into Practice* 21 (4): 293–300.

Hoyt, L. 2002. *Make It Real: Strategies for Success with Informational Texts.* Portsmouth, NH: Heinemann.

Huck, C. 1979. "Literature for All Reasons." *Language Arts* 55: 852–56.

International Reading Association. 2000. *Making a Difference Means Making It Different: Honoring Children's Rights to Excellent Reading Instruction.* Newark, DE: International Reading Association. Available online at *http://www.reading.org/positions/MADMMID.html.*

IRA/NCTE. 1996. *Standards for the English Language Arts.* Urbana, IL: IRA/NCTE.

Jenkins, C. 1999. *The Allure of Authors: Author Studies in the Elementary Classroom.* Portsmouth, NH: Heinemann.

Keene, E. O., and S. Zimmerman. 1997. *Mosaic of Thought: Teaching Comprehension in a Reader's Workshop.* Portsmouth, NH: Heinemann.

Kingsolver, B. 1999. *The Poisonwood Bible.* Paperback. New York: Perennial.

Kong, A., and P. D. Pearson. 2003. "The Road to Participation: The Construction of a Literacy Practice in a Learning Community of Linguistically Diverse Learners." *Research in the Teaching of English* 38 (1): 85.

Ladson-Billings, G. 1995. *The Dreamkeepers: Successful Teachers of African American Children.* San Francisco, CA: Jossey-Bass.

Loughlin, C. E., and M. D. Martin. 1987. *Supporting Literacy: Developing Effective Learning Environments.* New York: Teachers College Press.

Luna, C. S., J. Solsken, and E. Kutz. 2000. "Defining Literacy: Lessons from High-Stakes Teacher Testing." *Journal of Teacher Education* 51 (4): 276–88.

Martin, B. 1970. *Brown Bear, Brown Bear, What Do You See?* New York: Holt.

Massachusetts Department of Education. 2001. *Massachusetts English Language Arts Curriculum Framework.* Malden, MA: Massachusetts Department of Education.

McCormick, S. 1977. "Should You Read Aloud to Your Children?" *Language Arts* 54: 139–43.

Miller, L. 1993. *What We Call Smart: A New Narrative for Intelligence and Learning.* San Diego: Singular.

Mochizuki, K. 1995. *Baseball Saved Us*. Paperback. New York: Lee & Low.

Moustafa, M. 1997. *Beyond Traditional Phonics: Research Discoveries and Reading Instruction*. Portsmouth, NH: Heinemann.

Nathan, Jeff. 2003. *Calling All Animals: The First Book of PunOETRY™*. Paperback. Illustrated by Liz Ball. Andover, MA: Chucklebooks.

National Center for Education Statistics. 2003. *National Assessment of Educational Progress*. Washington, DC: National Center for Educational Statistics.

National Reading Panel. 2000. *Teaching Children to Read: An Evidence-Based Assessment of the Scientific Research Literature on Reading and Its Implications for Reading Instruction*. Washington, DC: National Institute of Child Health and Human Development. Available online at *www.nationalreadingpanel.org*.

Newkirk, T. 2002. *Misreading Masculinity: Boys, Literacy, and Popular Culture*. Portsmouth, NH: Heinemann.

Nieto, S. 1993. "We Have Stories to Tell: A Case Study of Puerto Ricans in Children's Books." Chapter 6 in *Teaching Multicultural Literature in Grades K–8*, edited by V. J. Harris, 55–108. Norwood, MA: Christopher-Gordon.

Offutt, C. 2002. *No Heroes: A Memoir of Coming Home*. New York: Simon & Schuster.

———. 1993. *The Same River Twice: A Memoir*. New York: Simon & Schuster.

Ogle, D. 1986. "KWL: A Teaching Model That Develops Active Reading of Expository Text." *The Reading Teacher* 39: 564–70.

O'Neill, A. 2002. *The Recess Queen*. New York: Scholastic.

Opitz, M. 1999. *Flexible Grouping in Reading (Grades 2–5)*. New York: Scholastic.

Pappas, C. C., B. Z. Kiefer, and L. S. Levstik. 1998. *An Integrated Language Perspective in the Elementary School: An Action Approach*. Boston: Addison-Wesley.

Park, B. 1982. *Skinnybones*. New York: Bullseye.

Pearson, D. 2001. Reading the Reading Reports: The Implications for Practice and Research of *Preventing Reading Difficulties in Young Children, The National Reading Report*, and *The Rand Reading*

Report. Paper presented at the Annual Meeting of the National Council of Teachers of English, November, Baltimore, MD.

———. 1997. "The First-Grade Studies: A Personal Reflection." *Reading Research Quarterly* 32: 428–32.

Pearson, D., and M. C. Gallagher. 1983. "The Instruction of Reading Comprehension." *Contemporary Educational Psychology* 8: 317–44.

Pintrich, P. R. 2002. "The Role of Metacognitive Knowledge in Learning, Teaching, and Assessing." *Theory into Practice* 41 (4): 220–27.

Rhodes, L. K., ed. 1993. *Literacy Assessment: A Handbook of Instruments.* Portsmouth, NH: Heinemann.

Rhodes, L. K., and C. Dudley-Marling. 1996. *Readers and Writers with a Difference: A Holistic Approach to Teaching Struggling Readers and Writers.* 2d ed. Portsmouth, NH: Heinemann.

Rhodes, L. K., and N. Shanklin. 1993. *Windows into Literacy: Assessing Learners, K–8.* Portsmouth, NH: Heinemann.

Roller, C. M. 1996. *Variability, Not Disability: Struggling Readers in a Workshop Classroom.* Newark, DE: International Reading Association.

Routman, R. 2003. *Reading Essentials: The Specifics You Need to Teach Reading Well.* Portsmouth, NH: Heinemann.

Savage, J. F. 2004. *Sound It Out! Phonics in a Comprehensive Reading Program.* Boston: McGraw Hill.

Scieszka, J. 1996. *The True Story of the Three Little Pigs.* Illustrated by L. Smith. New York: Puffin.

Sendak, M. 1988. *Where the Wild Things Are.* New York: HarperCollins.

Siegel, M. G. 1984. Reading as Signification. Ph.D dissertation, Indiana University, Bloomington.

Smith, F. 1998. *The Book of Learning and Forgetting.* New York: Teachers College Press.

———. 1981. "Demonstration, Engagement, and Sensitivity: A Revised Approach to Language Arts." *Language Arts* 58: 103–12.

Snow, C., M. S. Burns, and P. Griffin. 1998. *Preventing Reading Difficulties in Young Children: A Report of the National Research Council.* Washington, DC: National Academy Press.

Spinelli, J. 1998. *Wringer.* New York: HarperTrophy.

———. 1990. *Maniac Magee.* New York: Little Brown.

Steig, W. 1990. *Doctor De Soto.* New York: Sunburst.

Szymusiak, K., and F. Sibberson. 2001. *Beyond Leveled Books: Supporting Transitional Readers in Grades 2–5.* York, ME: Stenhouse.

Taberski, S. 2000. *On Solid Ground: Strategies for Teaching Reading K–3.* Portsmouth, NH: Heinemann.

Topping, K. 1989. "Peer Tutoring and Paired Reading: Combining Two Powerful Techniques." *The Reading Teacher* 42: 488–94.

———. 1987. "Peer-Tutored Paired Reading: Outcome Data from Ten Projects." *Educational Psychology* 7: 133–45.

Tsuchiya, Y. 1988. *Faithful Elephants: A True Story of Animals, People, and War.* Translated by T. T. Dykes. New York: Houghton Mifflin.

Weaver, C. 2002. *Reading Process and Practice.* 3d ed. Portsmouth, NH: Heinemann.

Wilhelm, J. D. 2001a. *Improving Comprehension with Think-Aloud Strategies: Modeling What Good Readers Do.* Jefferson City, MO: Scholastic Professional.

———. 2001b. *Guidelines and Student Handouts for Implementing Read-Aloud Strategies.* New York: Scholastic.

———. 1997. *"You Gotta Be the Book": Teaching Engaged and Reflective Reading with Adolescents.* New York: Teachers College Press.

Wuthrick, M. A. 1990. "Blue Jays Win! Crows Go Down in Defeat." *Phi Delta Kappan* 71: 553–56.

Yolen, J. 1992. *Encounter.* San Diego, CA: Harcourt, Brace, Jovanovich.

———. 1987. *Owl Moon.* New York: Philomel.

Index